MP5122

PASSPORT SERIES

AFRICA

Author: Heather Knowles
Contributors: Nancy Klepper
Editor: Jonathan Gross
Original Illustrations: Larry Nolte
Design and Layout: Kati Baker

Printed in the United States of America

ISBN 978-1-4291-2248-1

BRIDGING
the Gaps in Education™
Lorenz Educational Press
P.O. Box 802 • Dayton, OH 45401-0802
for other LEP products visit our website
www.LorenzEducationalPress.com

*All statistics are based on information from 2010.
**For further information on pronunciations, research foreign language dictionaries and/or the Internet.

Metric Conversions

The purpose of this page is to aid in the conversion of measurements in this book from the English system to the metric system. Note that the tables below show two types of ounces. Liquid ounces measure the volume of liquids and have therefore been converted into milliliters. Dry ounces measure weight and have been converted into grams. Because dry substances such as sugar and flour may have different densities, it is advisable to measure them according to weight rather than volume. The measurement unit of the cup has been reserved solely for liquid, or volume, conversions.

Conversion Formulas					
when you know	formula	to find			
		when you know	formula	to find	
teaspoons	× 5	milliliters	× .20	teaspoons
tablespoons	× 15	milliliters	× .60	tablespoons
fluid ounces	× 29.57	milliliters	× .03	fluid ounces
liquid cups	× 240	milliliters	× .004	liquid cups
U.S. gallons	× 3.78	liters	× .26	U.S. gallons
dry ounces	× 28.35	grams	× .035	dry ounces
inches	× 2.54	centimeters	× .39	inches
square inches	× 6.45	square centimeters	× .15	square inches
feet	× .30	meters	× 3.28	feet
square feet	× .09	square meters	× 10.76	square feet
yards	× .91	meters	× 1.09	yards
miles	× 1.61	kilometers	× .62	miles
square miles	× 2.59	square kilometers	× .40	square miles
Fahrenheit	$(°F - 32) × \frac{5}{9}$	Celsius	$(°C × \frac{9}{5}) + 32$	Fahrenheit

Equivalent Temperatures

32°F = 0°C (water freezes)
212°F = 100°C (water boils)
350°F = 177°C
375°F = 191°C
400°F = 204°C
425°F = 218°C
450°F = 232°C

Common Cooking Conversions

½ cup = 120 milliliters
12 fluid ounces = 354.88 milliliters
1 quart (32 ounces) = 950 milliliters
½ gallon = 1.89 liters
1 Canadian gallon = 4.55 liters
8 dry ounces (½ pound) = 227 grams
16 dry ounces (1 pound) = 454 grams

MP5122

Table of Contents

Botswana..4

Egypt 16

Kenya 34

Madagascar 48

Nigeria..60

Rwanda 71

Somalia 79

South Africa..88

Zimbabwe… 97

Answer Key… 108

Botswana

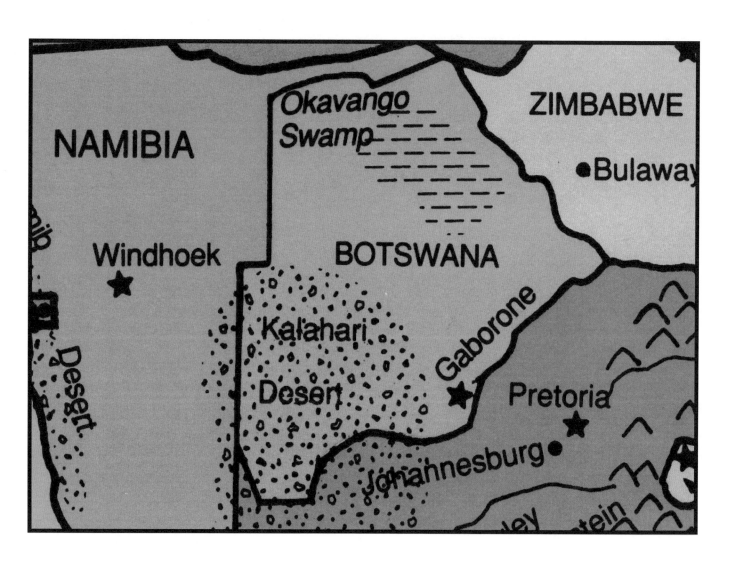

Welcome to Botswana!

Botswana, formerly the British Protectorate of Bechuanaland, is a landlocked country in southern Africa. The country is flat—70% of it being the Kalahari Desert. Since its independence in 1966, Botswana has risen from being one of the most impoverished countries in Africa to one of the most successful. Botswana's economy has developed and grown due to its diamond, tourism, and manufacturing industries.

FAST FACTS

Official Name: Republic of Botswana (*Lefatshe la Botswana*)

Location: Botswana is located in southern Africa, to the north of the country of South Africa.

Population: 2,029,307 (2010 estimate)

Capital City: Gaborone (also the largest city)

Area: 224,711 square miles

Major Languages: English, Setswana

Major Religions: Traditional religions and Christianity, as well as Islam, Hindu and Baha'is

Currency: The *pula*; 1 pula = 100 thebe

Climate: Botswana has a semiarid climate. The winters are warm and the summers hot.

The Land: Botswana features mostly flat or gently rolling tableland. The Kalahari Desert is found in the southwest.

Type of Government: Parliamentary Republic

Flag: The Botswana flag is light blue, with a horizontal black stripe across the middle. On either side of this black stripe is a small white stripe. The light blue color symbolizes rain and the white and black bands represent racial harmony.

Coat of Arms: The Botswana coat of arms features a traditional African shield, a zebra rearing on each side. The shield features three cogwheels, representing industry; three waves, symbolizing the country's need for water; and a bull's head that emphasizes the importance of cattle herding. Each of the zebras holds an item: on the left, an ivory tusk (once an important trade industry in Botswana); on the right, an ear of sorghum (a major crop in Botswana).

Official Animal: Zebra

Motto: "Pula" (Rain)

Natural Environment

Botswana is landlocked, surrounded by South Africa on the south and east, Namibia to the north and west, and Zimbabwe and Zambia to the northeast. Much of the land is low hills and rolling plains. The highest point, Tsodilo Hill (5,922 feet), is located in the northwestern corner of the country. The Okavango River is extremely important to the country, bringing vast amounts of water from the highlands of Angola to Botswana's dry regions. Instead of flowing into the sea, the Okavango River flows into a large depression known as the Okavango Swamp and Ngami Lake in the northern part of the Botswana plateau.

The western and southern two-thirds of the country are part of the large Kalahari Desert. The country experiences light rainfall and droughts, which vary from year to year in their severity. Most precipitation occurs in the summer, which takes place from October through April (since Botswana is located in the southern hemisphere). Summers are hot, with temperatures reaching 100 degrees Fahrenheit during the day. Winters are considerably cooler, with temperatures around or below freezing.

Dry scrub and small trees are located in the savanna regions of the north, and the desert is home to sparse thorn bushes. The vast amounts of sand and dry soil make agriculture virtually impossible. But the country has significant mineral deposits of diamonds, copper, coal and nickel.

Botswana is home to Blue Wildebeests, antelopes, African Wild Dogs, flamingos and other birds, and many mammals. One of the country's national parks, Chobe National Park, has the world's largest population of African elephants. The Chobe and other parks and reserves attract safari-taking tourists.

A HISTORY OF BOTSWANA

Botswana's modern history began around the end of the 18th century, when the Tswana people entered the territory and overtook the local people, called the San. During the 19th century, the country was invaded by several neighboring tribes. Khama III, chief of the Tswana's Bamangwato tribe, appealed to Britain for assistance. The British provided protection from the invaders. In 1885, this alliance established the British Protectorate of Bechuanaland.

In the early 20th century, rule was divided between British authority and an evolving tribal government. In 1934, tribal rule was regularized, though the British continued to consult and advise. In 1964, Britain accepted tribal proposals for a democratic self-government. In 1965, a constitution was enacted, which allowed general elections to take place. Botswana achieved independence on September 30, 1966, under the presidency of election-winner Seretse Khama.

In the years following independence, Botswana maintained no armed forces. Attacks by Rhodesian and South African troops, however, led to the formation of the Botswana Defense Force in 1977. The United States had a large role in the training and development of the organization's leadership. In the absence of military threat, the BDF focuses on disaster preparation, enforcement of poaching restrictions, and foreign peacekeeping. Ian Khama, son of Botswana's first president, resigned his leadership of the BDF in order to assume the presidency in 2008.

Botswana's economy is one of the fastest growing in the world. The country, one of the world's poorest countries at their independence, is now considered a middle-income country. Much of Botswana's economy is found in mining, particularly diamonds.

While the economy booms, Botswana's citizens face difficult challenges. Poverty and unemployment are high, and the developing education system has difficulty adequately training workers for the advanced economic conditions. The population is also being devastated by the AIDS pandemic. Botswana has one of the highest infection rates in the world, with approximately one in every six citizens affected. The young government is working hard to overcome these problems while continuing to lead Botswana to a promising future.

In Your Classroom

Using colorful paper or poster board and paints, have students make Botswana flags to hang in your classroom.

Draw a map of Botswana, labeling its major cities, rivers and desert. Make this map large enough to hang in the classroom so everyone can see it and use it for reference when discussing the country.

Daily Life

More than half of Botswana's population lives in rural areas. Many of these people farm only enough to feed themselves. Others raise livestock – primarily cattle, which is exported for profit. Some of the largest cities in Botswana include the capital of Gaborone, along with Francistown and Molepolole. There are still many *Bushmen* living in the country, though their population has dropped beneath 10,000. These people live in the wild as traditional hunter-gatherers.

Education

Since its independence, Botswana has made vast improvements to their education system. The discovery of diamonds and resultant economic wealth allowed the government to direct more efforts towards education. Students are guaranteed ten years of basic schooling, after which they are awarded a Junior Certificate. Secondary school is available, but not required; students must pay their own way, as well. After two years of secondary education, a Botswana General Certificate of Secondary Education is awarded.

The brightest students can continue at one of six technical colleges around the country. Two of the best and most popular of these, the University of Botswana, Botswana College of Agriculture and the Botswana Accountancy College, are located in Gaborone. Training schools are also a popular option for those with a secondary education certificate.

Entertainment

The people of Botswana can pass the time with natural pursuits. There is much to see in this beautiful country. Game and bird watching is common in places like the Okavango Delta and the Chobe Game Reserve. The environment provides numerous sightseeing and outdoor activity opportunities. At home, people can listen to radio stations or watch BTV (Botswana Television). They can also surf the Internet.

The Daily Life of Bushmen

Life is quite different for members of Bushmen tribes. This dwindling society lives off of the land and what nature provides. Villages are mobile, usually centered on a reliable source of water. Water is extremely important, as droughts can occur at any time. The men of a village do most of the hunting, though women sometimes participate, as well. Women gather other necessities, such as fruit, berries, and ostrich eggs. Many of the tribes have converted to agriculture-based societies as a result of the country's push for modernization.

Children are expected to play with one another, and little else. In fact, relaxation and recreation are important parts of Bushmen life. Much time is spent on conversation, music, and dance. Concepts of government and economy are more relaxed, with many village decisions made by consensus. The economy is often gift-based. Villagers will give one another important items on a regular basis, rather than trading or buying and selling.

Bushman for a Day

Bushmen like those living in Botswana can be found throughout southern Africa. Their way of life is very different from ours. Research the daily life of a Bushman (or Bushwoman). Learn what you can about their homes, their food, their activities, and more. Write about your findings in the first box below. In the second box, write about how you would feel growing up in a Bushmen community. Would you like it? Why or why not? What would be different about your daily routine? How would you handle those differences?

◇◇◇

Bushman Life

_____

_____

_____

_____

_____

_____

_____

My Bushman Life

_____

_____

_____

_____

_____

_____

_____

Language & Expressions

English is the official language of Botswana, though the tribal *Setswana* language is still widely spoken. In fact, the majority of the population speaks Setswana. One aspect that makes Setswana unique from many languages is the importance it places on prefixes. Setswana prefixes include "Bo"—referring to the country, "Mo"—referring to one person, "Ba"—referring to people, and "Se"—referring to the language. Take the name of the country, for example. The Tswana tribe is the main tribe. Adding the *Bo*- prefix applies the reference to the entire country, making *Botswana*.

Famous Botswana Proverbs

Here are some famous Botswana proverbs. What do you think they mean?

Eating without sharing is like swearing with your mouth.

Famine hides under the granary.

If you are too smart to pay the doctor, you had better be too smart to get sick.

Plenty is like the mist.

To give away is to make provision for the future.

Body Language and Etiquette in Botswana

Here are some examples of body language and etiquette you'll find in Botswana.

Always greet someone before asking for help, directions, or advice. Starting a conversation with a question is considered rude.

The handshake is an important element of social interaction, but it's a very specific kind of handshake. It consists of a traditional Western handshake, followed by a linking of bent fingers and upward-facing thumbs, and completed with a second Western handshake.

Botswanans believe revealing clothing is disrespectful. While in the country, wear conservative clothing, such as long pants, skirts, or shorts.

Do not take a photograph of a person without first asking permission – this is considered very rude. Also, be wary of any buildings you might want to photograph – government buildings may be restricted, for example.

Don't drive at night! Roaming wildlife and livestock make the roads extremely dangerous in the dark.

Know Before You Go

Here are some common phrases you will use in Botswana. Though English is likely to be understood by most Botswanans, speaking the Setswana language will impress and please most people.

English	Setswana
Hello, sir/madam.	Dumela, rra/mma.
How are you?	O tsogile jang? (formal)
	Le kae? (informal)
Bye.	Sharp. (pronounced *shup*)
Thank you.	Ke a leboga.
My name is ___.	Leina la me ke ___.
What is your name?	Leina la gago ke mang?
What time is it?	Ke nako mang?
Good night.	Boroko.

In Your Classroom

The Tswana are the main tribal group of the nation. Using what you have learned about their language, ask students what the following words mean: Botswana, Batswana, Setswana, and Motswana.

Have students apply Setswana prefixes to English. What would the name of their town or state be? What about their native language?

Botswanan food shares characteristics with other south African cuisine while establishing some unique dishes and practices.

Much of the food consumed in Botswana is from within the country. High-quality beef is raised, along with goat, lamb, mutton, chicken and fish. A variety of staple crops, vegetables, and fruits are grown by farmers. Beans are especially plentiful and popular. The watermelon is thought to have originated in Botswana, and is very popular when in season. Milk is the go-to beverage of choice, but local soft drink and beer factories provide tasty alternatives.

Popular Dishes

Pap
This staple of the Botswana diet is a thick porridge served with many dishes and side items. Most commonly, it is eaten at breakfast, usually with milk and sugar added. It is also consumed at other meals, complementing meats and onion and tomato stews.

Samp
This dish is made from corn kernels that are dried out, stamped, and chopped up. It is often served with beef, lamb, or chicken. Samp and beans is a very popular and common meal.

Vetkoek

Vetkoek is deep-fried dough stuffed with a variety of items; most commonly mince, or cooked beef. Other common fillings and toppings include honey, syrup, and jam.

Mopane Worms

You read correctly – worms. The mopane worm is a species of moth, and Botswanans love to collect and eat them while in the large caterpillar stage. An excellent source of protein, this unique treat, along with many species of insects, including grasshoppers, beetles, and termites, is eaten by Bushmen and city-dwellers alike. The mopane worm is eaten raw, soaked and fried, or flavored by tomato or chili sauce.

Holidays & Festivals

The Botswana population celebrates Christmas Day, Boxing Day, New Year's Day, Good Friday, Easter Monday and Ascension Day. On July 1, they celebrate Sir Seretse Khama Day, followed by President's Day on July 19. The country's independence is celebrated on September 30. They also celebrate several public holidays each year.

New Year's Day • *January 1*

Good Friday • *date varies*

Easter Monday • *date varies*

Ascension Day • *date varies*

Sir Seretse Khama Day • *July 1*

President's Day • *July 19*

Independence Day • *September 30*

Christmas • *December 25*

Boxing Day • *December 26/27*

Creative Arts

The earliest artistic endeavors in Botswana were paintings depicting hunting scenes. These paintings of animal and human figures are believed to have been created by Bushmen in the Kalahari Desert over 20,000 years ago.

The southeastern part of Botswana is known for its pottery and weaving. The women in the northern villages of Gumare and Etsha are well-known for their basket-making skills. To craft these baskets, the women use Mokola palms and locally-made dyes. They weave large baskets with lids used for storage, open baskets made for carrying supplies on one's head, and small baskets used for threshing grain. The colorful designs and delicate, durable craftsmanship make these baskets true art.

Along with these traditional arts, talented modern artists have also emerged from Botswana. Inspired by the country's beautiful landscape and people, their sculptures and paintings are on display in several galleries around Botswana.

Traditional Tswana music is primarily vocals accompanied by string instruments. Drums are never used. The traditional musical instruments they use include the *Setinkane* and the *Segankure/Segaba*. Recently, they have begun incorporating the guitar in their music.

In Your Classroom

Bring large amounts of modeling clay to class. Have students make miniature statues, sculptures, or pottery. Encourage them to be creative. Leave their completed artwork at school for several days until it has hardened. Once the clay is hard, let the students paint their creations. After they have been completed, put the artwork on display as you continue to discuss Botswana.

Botswana Art Response

Early art from Botswana exists in the hunting paintings of 20,000 years ago. Find some examples of these in books or on the Internet. Write your thoughts on the art on the lines below. Why did the painter create the scene? What does the scene show? How does it make you feel? Then create your own art in the box below – design something that is inspired by your research.

_____

_____

_____

_____

14

Sports & Games

Association football is the most popular sport in Botswana, followed by cricket. Other popular sports include tennis, rugby, softball, volleyball, and track and field.

Botswana first appeared in the 1980 Summer Olympic Games in Moscow, Russia. They have since competed in eight Olympics, none of which have been Winter Games. They have yet to win a medal. In 2004, however, Botswana sent Tshotlego Morama to the Summer Paralympics in Athens, Greece. She won a gold medal in the 400-meter sprint, setting a new world record time in the process.

Bridge is an extremely popular game among the people of Botswana. British expatriate school teachers brought the mind game to the Botswana classrooms several decades ago, and since then the game has spread all over the country. The Botswana Bridge Federation formed in the late 1980s and boasts over 800 members today. The organization still sponsors regular tournaments.

Egypt

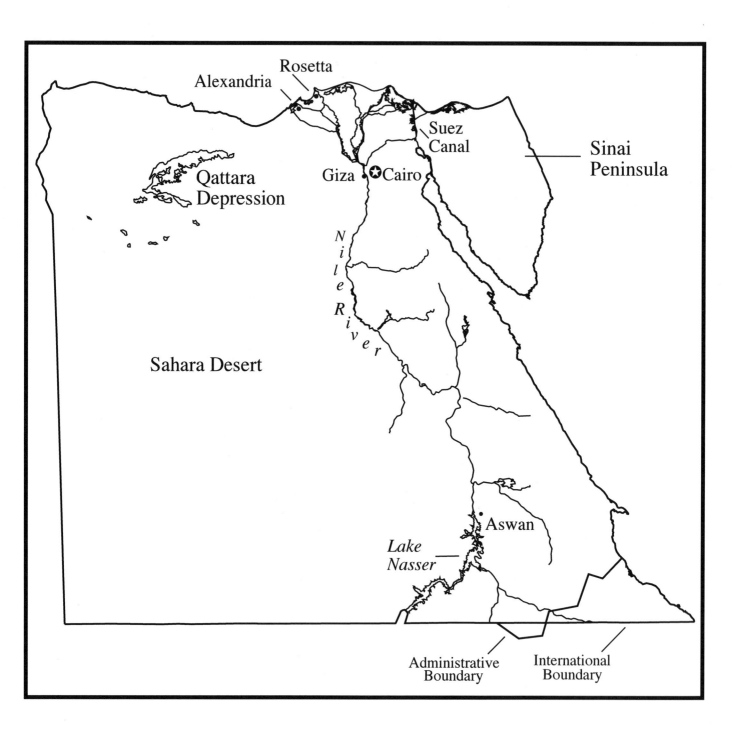

Alexandria

Rosetta

Qattara Depression

Suez Canal

Sinai Peninsula

Giza ⭐ Cairo

Nile River

Sahara Desert

Aswan

Lake Nasser

Administrative Boundary

International Boundary

Welcome to Egypt!

Archaeological records of ancient Egypt testify to a civilization which dates back to 4000 BCE This ancient society of African people is often referred to as the cradle of western civilization, and indeed Egypt is credited with many inventions and "firsts" that have propelled our world forward. Irrigation, the plow, linen, the 12–month calendar, and even the first paper are among the many contributions to civilization made by this respected African nation.

FAST FACTS

Official Name:	Arab Republic of Egypt (*Jumhriyah Misr al–Arabiya*)
Location:	Egypt is located in northern Africa, just south of the Mediterranean Sea. It is bordered by Libya on the west, Sudan on the south, and the Red Sea and the Gaza Strip on the east.
Population:	80,471,869 (2010 estimate)
Capital City:	Cairo
Area:	356,667 square miles Egypt is approximately the same size as Texas, Oklahoma, and Arkansas combined. Egypt is also similar in size to Nigeria, which claims 356,667 square miles.
Major Languages:	Arabic is the official language of Egypt. English and French are also spoken.
Major Religions:	Muslim (mostly Sunni): 90% Coptic: 9%
Currency:	the Egyptian pound
Climate:	Egypt has a desert climate. The summers are hot and dry. The winters are more moderate.
The Land:	Egypt is dominated by a desert plateau, with the Nile River valley and delta in the east.
Type of Government:	Republic
Flag:	The flag of Egypt is divided into three horizontal stripes. The red stripe at the top signifies the determination of the people. The middle white section represents the peaceful revolution which made the country a republic. The black stripe on the bottom is symbolic of the time before Egypt became a republic. Featured in the center of the white stripe is Egypt's coat of arms.
Coat of Arms:	Egypt's coat of arms portrays a gold eagle clutching the country's banner in its claws. The eagle symbolizes a Muslim warrior.
National Flower:	Lotus

RED
BLACK

GOLD
RED
BLACK

Natural Environment

Egypt is located in the northeastern portion of the African continent. It is bordered by Sudan to the south, Libya to the west, the Mediterranean Sea to the north, and Israel, the Red Sea, and Saudi Arabia to the east.

Egypt is a country of remarkable contrasts. Being home to both the world's largest desert, the Sahara, and the world's longest river, the Nile, Egypt offers vastly different climates within the same country. While 90 percent of Egypt is dry and arid desert, the Nile Valley is fertile, green, and lush. Temperatures range from 40°F (4°C) during the winter months to 100°F (38°C) in the summer months. Winters are mild, sunny, and dry. Many crops such as rice, beans, fruits, grains, vegetables, sugar, and corn are grown in Egypt. Egypt is one of the largest producers of cotton and the tenth-largest producer of cheese. Roughly half of all Egyptians are employed in agriculture and associated fields.

The Nile River
Proverb: Help yourself and the Nile will help you.

The Nile, at 4,160 miles long, is the world's longest river. Its width varies from 250 yards to 14 miles. It begins as two little rivers far to the south, the White Nile and the Blue Nile, which meet in Khartoum, Sudan. Most of Egypt's population lives along the Nile's banks or canals which extend from it.

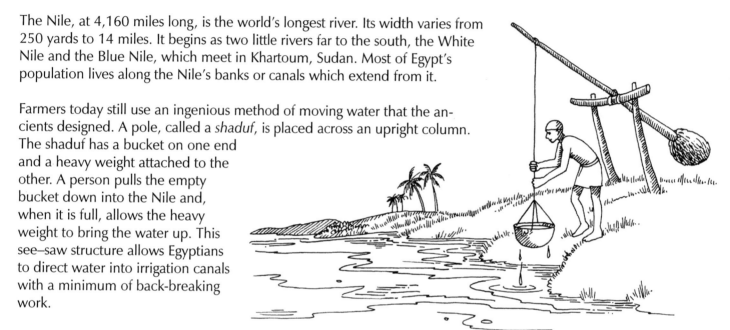

Farmers today still use an ingenious method of moving water that the ancients designed. A pole, called a *shaduf*, is placed across an upright column. The shaduf has a bucket on one end and a heavy weight attached to the other. A person pulls the empty bucket down into the Nile and, when it is full, allows the heavy weight to bring the water up. This see–saw structure allows Egyptians to direct water into irrigation canals with a minimum of back-breaking work.

The Suez Canal
The Suez Canal, located in the northeastern portion of Egypt, is a major man-made waterway which links the Mediterranean and Red Seas. The canal has been an important trade link between Europe and Asia ever since opening in 1869. The canal shortened the water route between Britain and India by 6,000 miles (9,660 kilometers). France supplied the majority of the funding for the project, as well as the engineer who designed the canal, and Egypt supplied the labor. Historically, the canal has been involved in many political disputes, closing down completely in two conflicts. Once, in 1956, the canal was closed for one year when Egypt nationalized the waterway. The second closing lasted from 1967 to 1975 in response to the war with Israel.

Cairo Earthquake
An earthquake measuring 5.9 on the Richter scale shook Cairo on October 12, 1992. While the tremor was only medium-size by world standards, the 40-second quake appeared more destructive than it would have been elsewhere because of the capital city's densely overcrowded neighborhoods, the rickety condition of much of the older housing, and the shoddy construction of some of the newer buildings.

Of the 6,452,000 inhabitants of Cairo, a high proportion of which are children, over 500 people were killed and more than 6,500 were injured. Many of these fatalities were children trampled to death in stampedes as residents scrambled into the streets.

18

In Your Classroom

Let students explore world maps and globes, and ask them to find Egypt. Make a game of asking questions about Egypt's location and physical features. (For example: "I'm thinking of a country that is east of Egypt.") Ask students to trace a map of Egypt onto tagboard. Using markers and paint, they can put in rivers, deserts, cities, and so on as they learn about them throughout the unit.

Working in small groups, students can design a flag for the classroom. When presenting it to their classmates, they can explain the significance of the colors and pictures on their flag.

On chart paper, record for the class a list of questions the students have about Egypt. Allow space to record the answers as they are discovered. Volunteers can research the information in the library.

Encourage students to use building materials such as blocks, ice cream bar sticks, and other commercially available products to construct a model of the shaduf and the irrigation system.

Hold a class discussion and construct a chart which compares the Nile to another important river system.

A HISTORY OF EGYPT

Archaeologists have discovered evidence of ancient Egyptian civilizations dating back to 4000 BCE. The earliest recorded history, however, begins about 3400 BCE, when King Menes of Upper Egypt conquered Lower Egypt and united the two to form the Old Kingdom. Thirty different dynasties, with kings, queens, emperors, empresses, and pharaohs, ruled Egypt for the next 3,000 years.

The Pyramid Age, peaking between 2900 and 2750 BCE, yielded the Giza Pyramids and many others that testify to the pharaohs' power and to the Egyptians' resourcefulness.

The Middle Kingdom, which existed from approximately 2500 BCE until 1580 BCE, was known for the escalation of foreign trade, mining in the Sinai Peninsula, and the building of a widespread irrigation system that increased productivity along the Nile River.

Because the fertile land of the Nile provided food and life in an otherwise barren region, Egypt was repeatedly invaded. Asian invaders were probably first, in 1650 BCE, followed by the Persians in 525 BCE. Alexander the Great brought Greek culture to Egypt in 332 BCE and named the land on which he settled "Alexandria," making this city the first capital of Egypt. The name *Egypt*, meaning "black land," came from the Greeks and referred to the fertile soil of the Nile. When Alexander died after only nine years of rule, one of his generals, Ptolemy, became pharaoh and began the dynasty that would once again assert Egypt as a powerful nation and respected culture. When Cleopatra, the last ruler of the Ptolemaic dynasty, committed suicide in 30 BCE, Egypt fell under Roman rule.

The year 640 CE brought the arrival of the Arabs and the Islamic religion, and the founding of Cairo as the capital of Egypt. Art and architecture flourished until the Turks succeeded in extending the Ottoman Empire to Egypt in 1517.

Napoleon controlled Egypt for the French from 1798 to 1801. A passing independent rule by Albanian-born Moham-med Ali was not successful economically. France and Britain vied for control of Egypt, motivated by the advantages of the Suez Canal, until Britain finally drove out the French and named Egypt a protectorate in 1914.

Official independence came in 1922 as a result of anti-British sentiments, but it was not until much later that Egyp-tians were really free. King Farouk I, who had reigned since 1936, was deposed in 1952, and Mohammed Naguib became premier. Egypt was declared a republic in 1953. One year later, Gamal Abdel Nasser ousted Naguib and di-rected Egypt through major reforms in education, industry, and banking, as well as through two wars with Israel and conflicts over the Suez Canal. When Nasser died in 1970, then Vice President Anwar al Sadat succeeded him. With Sadat as president, a peace treaty with Israel was signed in 1979. Sadat was assassinated by Muslim fundamentalists in 1981 and was succeeded by Hosni Mubarak.

Mubarak maintained autocratic rule for the next 30 years. In January of 2011, however, revolutions in other parts of the world started an inferno of protest and rebellion in Egypt, all directed against the dominating rule of President Mubarak. Centered in and around Cairo's Tahrir Square, the mostly peaceful protest grew in size and intensity as all the world watched. Despite his attempts to quell the rebellion, Mubarak stepped down after 18 days of constant protest. On February 11, he handed power over to the military, ending his three decades of rule. Change has arrived for the Egyptian people, but its effect upon the country and its relationships with the world are uncertain.

The Nubian Civilization

While evidence of the existence of black pharaohs and other black African-Egyptians is inconclusive, there is no dispute when the experts discuss the Nubian civilization. The Nubian people were definitely black Africans whose contributions to our world have only recently been appreciated.

Today the Nubians' land is southern Egypt and northern Sudan. The ancient boundary between Nubia and Egypt existed some 200 miles north of the present day Egypt-Sudan border. The region is arid and includes the land south of Aswan, Egypt, 1,000 miles from Khartoum, Sudan.

Recent discoveries and interest in the Nubian civilization have created a new field of archaeology, distinct from Egyp-tology. Nubia, less studied than Egypt, dates back 6,000 years and may have had an influence on Egypt's political system and the rise of the pharaohs. Lending credence to this theory is a stone incense burner excavated at Qustul, the capital of the Nubian Kingdom from 3800 to 3100 BCE. Now Qustul is an excavation site located just south of the Egyptian border in Sudan. A palace scene, including a ruler, a crown, and a falcon, is engraved upon the incense burner. Dated at 3100 BCE, the incense burner is the earli-est evidence yet found of pharaonic society.

From what archaeologists have been able to deduce from artifacts, Egypt dominated Nubia for approximately 1,200 years, followed by nearly a century of Nubian rule over Egypt. During the reign of the Nubian civilization, Egyptian society flourished, producing valuable art and impressive temples.

One such temple, the temple at Abu Simbel, was dismantled, moved, and reconstructed in order to save it from the flood waters created by the Aswan Dam. The cities, roads, and palaces built by the Nubians are similar to those of the Egyptians, and some are even more advanced.

The Nubians had a system of writing called *Meroitic* which has been only partially deciphered. A 2,000-year-old sandstone tablet, inscribed with Egyptian and Meroitic writings, has helped to decipher part of this system. Other pieces of the tablet are needed to translate the writings completely.

20

In Your Classroom

As the students learn about the history of Egypt, have them illustrate and write about certain events, such as the Pharaohs' rule, the building of the pyramids, invasions, and the beginning of Islam. The individual work can then be displayed as a timeline. Compare sections of the Egyptian timeline with a timeline for North America.

Have small groups of students act out important historical events of Egypt, and sequence the individual acts into a play.

Explain to students how archaeologists excavate the earth to find artifacts which give them clues about ancient civilizations. *Archaeologist* is a term derived from the Greek words *archaeo*, meaning "early times" or "beginnings," and *logos*, meaning "theory" or "science." Discuss how archaeologists must dig very patiently and carefully so as not to damage any objects they might find. Provide students with a large box filled with dirt and sand in which you have hidden some small treasures. The students will enjoy "excavating" these artifacts.

Ancient Egyptian Gods and Goddesses

The gods and goddesses were very real to the ancient Egyptians. Over 3,000 deities represented different aspects of life and nature.

Use reference sources to match the names of the gods and goddesses with their descriptions.

Amun	Anubis	Geb	Hathor
Horus	Isis	Nut	Osiris
Ra	Seth	Shu	Thoth

Name	**Description**
1. _____	The creator god portrayed with the head of a ram
2. _____	Goddess of love, music, and dance sometimes pictured as a crow
3. _____	Sky goddess
4. _____	Earth god
5. _____	God of air who held up the sky
6. _____	God of the dead, often portrayed as mummified
7. _____	Ruler of the desert, storms, and violence portrayed with a forked tail and the head of a greyhound
8. _____	Moon god; also god of wisdom and writing with a bird-shaped (ibis) head
9. _____	Son of Osiris and Isis, often portrayed with the head of a falcon
10. _____	Queen of the gods represented as wearing a headdress and usually sitting on a throne
11. _____	The jackal-headed god of embalming
12. _____	Sun god with a large circle representing the sun over his falcon head

Egypt – MP5122

Daily Life

Family Life

Although the Egyptian household traditionally included two to three generations, increased urbanization has changed the modern family unit into a husband, wife, and unmarried children. Elders are revered and supported well by their adult children. Adult Egyptians gladly turn to their parents for guidance with major decisions, even such decisions as whom to marry. The father is the head of the family.

Clothing

People living in the city with above-average incomes wear western clothing. Poor people and rural villagers wear more traditional clothing. Traditional dress for men is a long-sleeved, loose-fitting shirt called a *galabiyah* ("gal-a-bia"), which reaches the ankles. Long white trousers are worn underneath the galabiyah, and a felt skullcap is worn on the head. More traditional women wear hooded black robes called *mylayas* ("mi-la-yas"), which cover their hair and bodies but not their faces. Although modest western clothing is widely accepted, shorts, low necklines, sleeveless blouses, and short skirts are not considered tasteful dress, even for visitors.

Work Schedule

In Egypt, people in business generally work from 8:30 AM to 2:00 PM, and then again from 5:30 to 9:00 PM. This pattern helps to avoid exertion during the midday heat, especially in the summer months. In open-air markets or bazaars, called *suqs*, one might find buyers and sellers negotiating over prices. Friday is the day of worship for Muslims, and all banks, stores, schools, and government offices are closed.

General Attitudes

In comparison to westerners, Egyptians favor a more relaxed attitude about life. They appear undaunted by time constraints and pressures typical in American culture. *Inshallah*, or "If God wills it," is a common response to any uncertainty, reflecting Muslims' reliance on God and their belief that Allah directs every aspect of their lives. If one was to generalize about the Egyptian personality, a good sense of humor and a very expressive manner would be traits at the top of the list.

Egyptian Cities and Villages

The capital of Egypt is Cairo is a modern city with a large population. *Cairo* is an Arabic word meaning "the victorious." Cairo is a typical large city. In addition to the skyscrapers and busy streets, however, Cairo also has some 250 *mosques* (Muslim houses of worship), with their *minarets* (towers) dominating the city's skyline. Cairo is the home of one of the oldest schools in the world, Al-Azhar University, which is one thousand years old. Today, Cairo is the seat of the Arab League, an organization of Middle Eastern and African nations that originated in 1945 to help settle disputes peacefully. Egypt was one of the first seven member nations of the Arab League.

Mosque with minarets

Alexandria is another large city in Egypt. It was named for Alexander the Great, one of the most influential of Egypt's long line of conquerors. Its proximity to both the Nile River and the Mediterranean Sea makes Alexandria an important port and link to the rest of the world.

Half of Egypt's population lives in small towns and villages spread throughout Egypt along the banks of the Nile. Peasants living in these rural areas are called *fellahin,* and they make their living by tending livestock or farming small areas of land for richer landowners. Buildings and homes are built from mud bricks and have thatched straw roofs.

Visitors may see goat herds wandering the streets or camels being used as transportation or work animals. Village life centers on work and the practice of Islam.

In Your Classroom

Students may enjoy incorporating their new knowledge of Egyptian culture into a short story or illustrated comic strip. When students share their work with the class, be sure to have them explain the new information they have included.

Find Cairo and Alexandria on a map of Egypt. Brainstorm a list of reasons why the ancient Egyptians would choose to begin towns in these two places. Add the cities to the class map, marking Cairo with a star because it is the capital. Compare the populations of these two cities with those of two large cities in your area.

Use travel brochures to plan a trip to Egypt. The students may decide which places they would like to visit, and then plan a detailed itinerary, mapping out their travel route.

Use clay to construct models of camels, depicting their role in Egyptian life.

Language & Expressions

Famous Egyptian Proverbs

Here are some famous Egyptian proverbs. What do you think they mean?

A monkey is a gazelle in its mother's eyes.
Time never gets tired of running.
Cover your candle. It will light more.
Stretch your legs as far as your quilt goes.
Give Saturday, you will find Sunday.

Body Language and Etiquette in Egypt

Here are some examples of body language and etiquette you'll find in Egypt.

It's best to wear conservative clothing in Egypt. Long pants and shirts that cover the shoulders and upper arms are appropriate attire.

Placing your right hand over your heart symbolizes gratitude. It's also a polite way to say "no."

Do not hold your palm out towards someone. This gesture is meant to ward off evil, and is offensive when presented to someone's face.

It is considered impolite to show the soles of your feet or shoes. Be mindful of how you sit.

If you're a guest for an Egyptian meal, expect to be offered food and/or drinks frequently. It is customary to accept after a few offers, rather than right away.

The Arabic Language

Arabic is the official language of Egypt and many other Middle Eastern countries. It consists of many different dialects. The dialect of Cairo is the most commonly used dialect throughout Egypt. Arabic is a modern descendant of the language of the Qur'an.

Arabic Expressions*
Ma'aleesh ("Don't worry about it; never mind.")
Inshallah ("If God wills it, it will happen.")
al Salamu Alaykum (el sa–LA–moo ALAY–kum) ("Peace be with you.")

The following is how one would write this greeting in Arabic:

*Remember that you read and write Arabic from right to left!

Many English words are of Arabic origin. Examples include the following:

English	Arabic
adobe	al tuba
camel	jamal
sesame	simsim
sugar	sukkar

Arabic Numbers

| 1 | 2 | 3 | 4 | 5 | 6 | 7 | 8 | 9 | 0 |

Hieroglyphics

The ancient Egyptians created a system of writing called *hieroglyphics* in which pictures were used to represent words. Hieroglyphics utilizes over 700 different signs, or hieroglyphs, that come from one of three categories. There are signs that stand for one sound; for example, a zigzag line represents the /n/ sound, and a half circle represents the / t/ sound. Other signs can stand for two or more sounds, similar to digraphs in the English language. For example, an open rectangle represents /pr/. Still another group of pictures, called *determinatives*, do not represent sounds at all. Instead, they just picture the whole word. A picture of a man with his arms tied behind his back is the symbol for enemy. Vowel sounds are not represented at all.

This cartouche of King Unas, the last king of the Fifth Dynasty, reads from left to right.

Cartouches are the curved lines that frame the names of the pharaohs. Using reed pens and brushes dipped in black and red ink, scribes enjoyed a privileged social status as they were needed to translate the complicated system to others. It is thought by some that the scribes may have intentionally kept their writing confusing to maintain their superiority. However, two lesser forms of hieroglyphics were developed: *hieratic*, which was a simpler, cursive form of hieroglyphics, and *demotic*, which was meant especially for the common people. Hieroglyphics could be written left to right, right to left, or top to bottom.

The Rosetta Stone

The Rosetta stone has been the key to unlocking the meaning of Egyptian hieroglyphics. It is a piece of black basalt, measuring three feet, nine inches long, two feet, four inches wide, and 11 inches thick. It was found in 1799 near the mouth of the Nile, and it was named for the nearby town, Rosetta. The inscriptions on the stone are hieroglyphic, demotic, and Greek. Thomas Young, an Englishman, and Jean-François Champollion, a French archaeologist, working independently of each other, were able to use the Greek inscriptions to decipher the hieroglyphics. In 1822, twenty-three years after its discovery, the Rosetta stone provided historians with a tool for reconstructing Egypt's ancient history. The inscriptions on the stone explain the reign of Ptolemy V and date back to the year 195 BCE. It was carved to show appreciation to Ptolemy V for favors he had done for the priests.

In Your Classroom

Students will enjoy making up their own hieroglyphics to tell a story. Make several copies of the hieroglyphs or make a chart for the children to refer to. Lead the class in creating a hieroglyphic message before allowing them to create their own. Students can use spoons or rounded scissors to "carve" their hieroglyphics into styrofoam (meat trays work well). Watercolor brushes dipped in diluted poster paint work well also.

Name _____ Date _____

Egyptian Writing

At first, Egyptian writing consisted of small pictures called hieroglyphs. Each picture represented a word or idea. However, that type of writing could be confusing when recording complex ideas.

A picture like this could stand for a person's foot. It also could mean walking, traveling, running, or other action words.

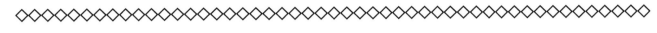

1. For each picture, write three possible meanings.

A. _____   B. _____   C. _____

_____   _____   _____

_____   _____   _____

Eventually the pictures came to stand for specific sounds instead of whole words. Only special scholars called scribes learned to read and write.

2. Draw small pictures to represent the following words.

man   woman   food

many   river   hot weather

3. Use your own ideas to write these sentences in pictures.

   A. *The man walked for three days across the desert.*

   B. *The crops were better last year than this year.*

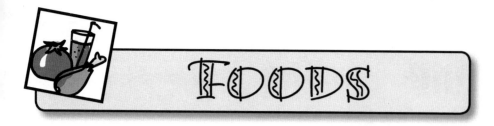

FOODS

Foods common in Egypt include rice, bread, fish, lamb, chicken, turkey, and stuffed vegetables. *Tahini* (a sesame seed paste), tomatoes, yogurt, and cucumbers are the usual relishes at every meal. A traditional Egyptian meal would include fava beans, chick peas with tahini, and flat Egyptian bread called *pita bread*. Pork and alcohol are prohibited for followers of Islam.

Egyptian Yogurt Salad
2 cups raisins
2 cups walnuts
2 large containers plain yogurt
2 medium-sized cucumbers (peeled and diced)
1 tablespoon fresh dill (crushed)
1 tablespoon fresh mint (crushed)
1 teaspoon lemon juice

Mix ingredients in a bowl. Serve chilled. Egyptian Yogurt Salad serves 20 to 25, allowing for small portions.

Falafel Balls
Falafel is a high-protein food eaten throughout the Middle East. It is made from ground chickpeas and fava beans. It is convenient to pack for trips across the desert because it can be stored dry and is quickly rehydrated.

Falafel balls can easily be made from a packaged falafel mix available in many supermarkets and health food stores. After following the recipe supplied in the package, you may want to experiment with different sauces for dipping. *Tahini* sauce can be made by blending one cup tahini, ½ cup water, ½ cup lemon juice, garlic, and salt. For a creamy sauce, mix one cup plain yogurt with ½ cup of blue cheese dressing, one teaspoon olive oil, and a dash of salt.

Eating Customs and Etiquette

If invited to someone's home to dine, a visitor may be overwhelmed by the amount of food which is offered. The overabundance is a measure of the host's generosity, and custom dictates that some food be left on your plate as a compliment. Another sign of respect in Egypt and other Arab nations is the serving of coffee. The cup will be filled to the brim to show the host's overflowing hospitality, and to refuse it is an insult. Food should only be eaten with the right hand as usage of the left hand alone is considered rude. Dinner may not be served until 10:30 PM or later. Invited guests usually bring a gift of flowers or chocolates. It is important not to admire the possessions of your host too much. Arab custom dictates that a host must please the guests, even if it involves giving away his or her own things. In Egypt, it is customary to address people by their title and their first name unless otherwise instructed. Greetings are usually offered warmly, and an enthusiastic response is expected in return. Polite guests will not begin business talk until pleasantries and friendly conversation have been exchanged. When sitting, the soles of the shoes and the feet should point downward and be kept hidden from view; it is considered an insult to do otherwise.

In Your Classroom

Have an Egyptian meal with a few students designated as the hosts and the others as the guests. Conduct the visit and meal following Arab etiquette.

Holidays & Festivals

Egypt celebrates a number of national, public, and religious holidays. As Islam is the official religion, all Islamic holidays are celebrated by the entire country. Egyptians of every religion join in celebrating the country's many festivals and carnivals, usually recognizing a saint.

National and Public Holidays

Christmas • *January 7* • Celebrated in January, this holiday celebrates the birth of Jesus Christ.

National Police Day • *January 25* • Egyptians celebrate their national police force.

Sinai Liberation Day • *April 25* • This day commemorates the withdrawal of Israeli troops from the Sinai Peninsula in 1982.

Labour Day • *May 1* • This holiday recognizes the economic and social achievements of workers.

Revolution Day • *July 23* • This day celebrates the anniversary of the 1952 revolution.

Armed Forces Day • *October 6* • Egypt remembers their troops crossing the Suez Canal during the October War.

Sham El Nessim • *date varies* • This day marks the beginning of spring.

Islamic New Year • *date varies* • Celebrated on the first day of the new year, this holiday is based on the Islamic Calendar.

Birthday of the Prophet Muhammad • *date varies* • This day celebrates the birthday of the prophet Muhammad, the founder of Islam.

Eid al-Fitr • *date varies* • This three-day celebration marks the breaking of the fast of Ramadan.

Eid al-Adha • *date varies* • This celebration marks the end of the Hajj and commemorates the sacrifice of Abraham.

Crafts

Just as the pyramids attest to the Egyptians' remarkable building and engineering skills, their jewelry is evidence of beautiful and artistic craftsmanship. Gold and silver were used to make fabulously ornate necklaces, bracelets, rings, and earrings. Many semiprecious gems such as amethyst, cornelian, quartz, and feldspar were obtained by trading with Afghan merchants. *Lapis lazuli*, a brilliant blue gem, was especially prized because the Egyptians thought the hair of the sun god, Ra, was made from it.

Jewelry was often designed around religious beliefs. For example, King Tut had a pair of four-inch earrings designed featuring cobras, which were believed to ward off evil spirits. The *scarab*, the sacred Egyptian beetle, was often the center of jewelry design. Real beetles were observed to push balls of dung around, and the Egyptians thought the sun was pushed across the sky in the same way. The scarab came to symbolize the sun god, Ra, and was seen as a symbol of protection and good luck. A scarab was always placed over the heart of the deceased king to help him pass the tests in the Underworld. Another symbol used in jewelry designs was the *ankh*, a cross with a loop on top, which symbolized life. Only kings and queens were allowed to wear the ankh, since they were thought to be capable of giving life and taking it away.

The ancient Egyptians developed a method of making paper from the papyrus plant which grew in the marshes along the banks of the Nile. Inner layers were cut into strips, pressed together, rubbed with smooth stones, and dried in the sun. The resulting paper was rolled into long cylinders when not in use.

Ankh

Scarab beetle bracelet

Music and Dance

In ancient Egypt, music and dance were featured during every celebration and festival, even funerals. Instruments such as flutes, harps, pipes, lutes, and lyres were used as accompaniment. Magicians and storytellers were important entertainers.

In modern-day Egypt, followers of Islam do not honor saints, but it is permissible to recognize holy men, especially in the south. On special occasions, festive ceremonies are performed near the tombs of holy men. A religious dance, called the *zikr*, involves dancers whirling around the tomb seven times.

A sculpture of King Mycerinus of the Fourth Dynasty and his queen.

Art

Egyptian art has given us a lot of information about the daily lives and religious beliefs of the ancient Egyptians. Sculptures were carved out of wood, copper, bronze, gold, and stone. Bright colors were commonly used in paintings. Paintings of people were almost always done with the person's chest and shoulders facing forward and the face depicted in profile. Egyptian artists mixed frontal and profile views because they were eager to portray as much information about their subjects as possible. Because of the strong connection between art and religion, Egyptians were reluctant to experiment with art forms. Tomb paintings were colored in vivid blues, greens, yellows, and reds. Scenes of everyday life and pictures illustrating what a person hoped to do in the afterlife were common.

Architecture

The Pyramids
*"The glory of the King is in the sky, his power is in the horizon." (the **Pyramid Texts**)*

The pyramid of Khufu in Egypt, called the Great Pyramid, is one of the Seven Wonders of the World. Certainly all of the pyramids make us wonder! Approximately 5,000 years old, the pyramids are the oldest stone structures found anywhere. The Great Pyramid at Giza stands 480 feet tall—taller than the Statue of Liberty—and covers an area greater than that of ten football fields. Amazingly, more than 80 pyramids still stand today, leading us to imagine an intelligent and highly-developed civilization.

Archaeologists can only theorize about how these massive and precise structures were built without benefit of modern machinery. It is estimated that it required the diligent work of 100,000 people, across a span of 20 years, to construct just one pyramid. Each limestone block in a pyramid weighs more than two tons, and the largest pyramid was constructed with over two million blocks. The limestone and granite were quarried close to the banks of the Nile, then transported to the pyramid site in wooden boats. It is thought that huge wooden rollers, and a lot of ingenuity, moved the stones along a causeway from the water's edge to the pyramid. Because the pyramids were built to serve as tombs for dead kings, the causeway doubled as a path for the funeral procession after the pyramid's completion. The Egyptians, using only copper tools and wooden wedges and levers, were able to cut and fit the stones so precisely that not even the blade of a knife could fit between them. The builders were careful that each side of the pyramid faced a particular direction, and that the base was perfectly level. This was all done without the aid of a compass or a level. Intricate false passages and imposing granite doors were constructed to protect the king's body and possessions from thieves.

The Step Pyramid was the first pyramid completed. It was built for King Djoser in 2630 BCE by his architect, Imhotep. The six stages, or steps, were meant to serve as a stairway for the king to join Ra, the sun god, in the sky. The true pyramid, with sloping sides, was developed later and was meant to represent the original mound of earth that rose from the water in the beginning of time. The sphinx, a half-human and half-lion creature, was constructed, many times in pairs, to protect the approaches to the pyramids and temples. The Great Sphinx is the largest, oldest, and most famous sphinx statue. It lies in the desert by Giza.

The Step Pyramid

The Great Sphinx

Building the pyramids may have been tedious, often dangerous work, yet some archaeologists theorize that the Egyptians were happy to risk their lives building both a tomb and a monument for their king. In addition to believing that the pharaohs were sons of Ra, the sun god, ancient Egyptians had a strong belief in life after death. They believed in the afterlife because they witnessed the "death" of the sun each day and its "rebirth" the following morning. The Nile, too, suggested rebirth, for every year it flooded and enriched the soil. A king, or *pharaoh* (which means "great house"), entombed in a glorious pyramid, could continue to bring honor and good fortune to the people. The shape of the pyramids was important because they were believed to be staircases to the heavens. The angles of the sides had to match exactly those of the sun's rays descending from the sky at twilight.

Although the pharaohs went to great lengths to ensure that their bodies and possessions were protected by the pyramids, robbers have ransacked nearly all of them. One tomb, however, that of Pharaoh Tutankhamen, was discovered almost untouched by archaeologist Howard Carter in 1922 after a seven-year search. Pharaoh Tutankhamen, more often referred to as King Tut, became a king at the age of nine and died when he was only nineteen. Many of the treasures discovered in his tomb were made of solid gold, among them a mask that shows his African facial features. Two wooden coffins encased King Tut's coffin, which was made from 2,500 pounds of gold.

In Your Classroom

Make rings and bracelets with your students. Metal tooling sheets can be purchased in art supply stores. The sheets are easily cut with scissors and flexible enough to bend into rings or bracelets. Pieces of bright tissue paper can be glued on to simulate gems.

After examining some examples of Egyptian art, have students design and paint a mural depicting Egyptian life. Students can trace around their own body shapes and do head profiles to model the Egyptian style.

Borrow recorders or flutes and any stringed instruments from the music department. Students will enjoy creating their own Egyptian music.

After reading some Egyptian tales to students, encourage them to retell a story using their own words and adding body movements and hand gestures.

A nearby art museum may have an Egyptian art display worth visiting. Some museums even offer kits you may borrow to share with your students.

Hold a short class discussion on western burial customs as compared to those of the ancient Egyptians. Students may be interested to discover that the Mound Builders, a Native American culture, built their mounds for the same purpose as the pyramids during the same time period.

Students can make a map of a pyramid, including the inside chambers, the intricate passages, and the causeway on the outside.

Sports & Games

Egypt enjoys a well-earned international reputation for excellence in several sports. Football (soccer) is easily the most popular national sport. Several talented teams compete for the title of the best team in Egypt. It's not uncommon for victorious fans to take to the streets after big victories. The Cairo Derby, a soccer match between two of Africa's finest football squads, is known as one of the toughest derbies in the world.

Egyptians enjoy and excel at the sports of tennis, squash, and handball. Egyptian teams and players have performed extremely well in international competitions since the early 1900s.

Squash equipment

Although many Egyptian games and activities are similar to those found in western societies, some activities remain gender-biased. For example, only girls play with dolls and only boys pretend to be soldiers. Paintings, murals, and artifacts portray the games and activities ancient Egyptians enjoyed. Many of these pastimes still survive today.

Khuzza lawizza is played like leapfrog with partners jumping over each others' backs.

Chelik-Chcmah is a game very similar to baseball, but the bat used is just a long stick.

A favorite game worldwide is playing catch. It is made trickier in Egypt when the players ride piggyback on their partners. Clay balls with seeds inside add a musical twist.

Senet (also called *zenet*) is a game closely resembling checkers. It involves moving pieces on a square board. Although a game, senet symbolizes the journey the dead must successfully complete in order to reach the Field of Reeds and luxuriate in the kingdom of Osiris. The board contains three rows of ten squares, each with a different picture engraved on it. The pictures show advantages and dilemmas which would put the player closer to, or farther from, the Field of Reeds. The ancient Egyptians decided their "moves" by throwing sticks. Today's players use dice.

Wari (also called *mancala*) is a common board game played by both Egyptian children and adults. People can be seen playing wari in cafés in Cairo where the loser will buy the coffee for his or her opponent. It is considered a man's game, and although women do play, no man wants to run the risk of losing to a woman and having to endure the teasing of his friends. We know wari was played by the ancients, as boards have been found carved in the stone of some pyramids and temples. Various forms of this game are played around the world and are known by many names.

The wari board is divided into 14 compartments, six on each side, and one at either end to hold captured pieces. The playing pieces can be nuts, dry beans, or small stones. The object of the game is to capture the opponent's pieces.

Kenya

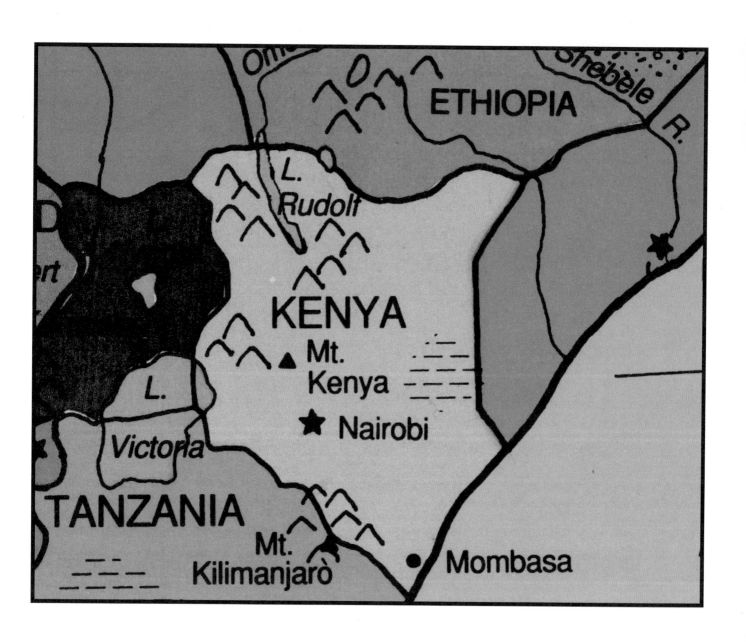

Welcome to Kenya!

Kenya is a beautiful country in east Africa, bordering the Indian Ocean. The country is known for its diverse topography and variety of wildlife. Since Kenya is located on the equator it experiences very little seasonal changes, making it an ideal spot for tourists to vacation year-round. The scenery is not, however, the only beautiful element of this country. The history and culture is as vibrant as the blue sky and zebra stripes!

FAST FACTS

Official Name: Republic of Kenya

Location: Kenya is found in eastern Africa, bordered by Ethiopia to the north, Uganda to the west, Tanzania to the south, and Somalia to the east. The Indian Ocean borders Kenya on the southeastern corner.

Population: 40,046,566 (2010 estimate)

Capital City: Nairobi

Area: 225,080 square miles

Major Languages: English and Kiswahili (Swahili)

Major Religions: Protestant: 45%
Roman Catholic: 33%
Muslim: 10%
Indigenous beliefs: 10%

Currency: Kenyan shilling

Climate: Along the coast, Kenya experiences a tropical climate. Inland, an arid climate dominates.

The Land: A major feature of Kenya is the Great Rift Valley in the central highlands. Low plains and a fertile plain are other elements.

Type of Government: Republic

Flag: The Kenyan flag is made up of four colors: black, symbolizing the country's black majority; red, symbolizing bloodshed during the country's struggle for independence; green, for Kenya's natural wealth; and white, for peace. The horizontal black, red and green stripes are separated by two thin white stripes between the black and the red and also between the red and the green. A traditional red, white, and black shield and two spears are located in the center of the flag.

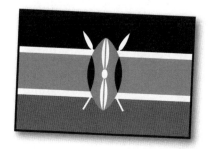

Coat of Arms: The Kenyan coat of arms features two lions, symbolic of protection, holding spears across a tribal shield (symbolizing unity and defending freedom) containing the country's colors – black, red, green, and white. The shield also features a rooster holding an axe, a symbol of prosperity.

National Motto: "Harambee!" ("Let's work together!")

Natural Environment

Kenya is bordered by Ethiopia and Somalia to the north and northeast, Tanzania on the south, Uganda and Lake Victoria on the west, and Sudan to the northwest. The Indian Ocean lies to the east, lining Kenya's coast with coral reefs, sand banks, mangrove swamps, coconut palms, coral beaches, and various islands. Some of the larger islands are: Lamu, Manda, and Mombasa.

Inland, Kenya is home to the dry Taru Plains and the Tana River Valley, a desert. The country also has numerous lakes, such as Lake Turkana and Lake Victoria—Africa's largest lake. Africa's tallest mountain, Mount Kilimanjaro (19,341 ft), is also located in Kenya. The country gets its name from Mount Kenya, also located there, which is the second tallest mountain in Africa. The Great Rift Valley also adds variety to Kenyan topography. In this region, one can find faults in the earth's crust, sinking spots and volcanoes which are mostly inactive.

Kenyan temperatures depend on the region's altitude. Atop the tall mountains, temperatures can be sub-zero. Monsoon winds called *Kaskazi* cool the coast from November to March. The rest of the year, winds from the southeast, called *Kusi*, cool the area.

The coastal region experiences tropical sunshine, while the jungles experience violent, heavy downpours of rain. The highlands of Kenya are mostly hot and sunny. The country experiences two rainy seasons per year: the long rains between March and June and the short rains in November. Although it usually does not rain all day long, when rain falls, it leaves the roads muddy and dangerous.

Since the equator is so close, the country does not have typical seasons. The sun almost always rises at six in the morning and sets around seven in the evening, year round. Kenyans keep track of time by beginning to count the hours from when the sun rises. Sunrise and sunset are both zero.

The country is home to a diverse collection of wildlife including rhinoceros (*faru*), elephants, giraffes (*twiga*), zebras (*pundamilia*), buffalos, hippopotamuses (*kiboko*), cheetahs (*duma*), leopards (*chui*), hyenas (*fisi*), crocodiles (*mamba*), and ostriches. Many tourists come to take safaris and watch these animals from the safety of a moving vehicle.

Many beautiful flowers grow throughout the country. Hibiscus, frangipani, Bougainvillea, jacaranda and Nandi Flame are some of the unique plants you might see. Kenya is also riddled with bamboo, forests, papyrus plants, baobab trees, palms along the coast, and acacias in the savannas.

Unfortunately, urbanization is endangering much of Kenya's wildlife. Animals' natural habitats are being destroyed and plant life is dwindling. People are making an attempt to conserve and preserve these animals and plants by setting up wildlife reserves, but harm is still being done.

In Your Classroom

If you have a continental map of Africa available, have students them identify the country. Then students can make a large map of Kenya. Students should color the map based on the physical features of Kenya's different regions. Have them clearly identify the major cities and rivers.

Draw a Kenyan flag and hang it in a prominent location in the classroom; or have students make their own flags and keep them in an organized folder with other Kenya materials.

Discuss how humanity often harms the environment. Challenge students to brainstorm ways to avoid the damage. Explain to the students that this takes place in other countries, as well, and discuss specific examples.

Chart the sunrise and sunset in your area. If you are not awake to see the sunrise, you can check a local weather station for information. Keep track of what time the sun rises and sets each day for two or more weeks. Do you see a change from when you started charting the times? Discuss how the earth's rotation affects our sunrises and sunsets. Why does it not affect Kenya in the same way?

To illustrate the activity above, and other aspects of being located on the equator, have one student hold a globe. Have another student shine a lamp or flashlight on the equator. As the student rotates the globe as the earth would rotate on its axis, discuss why countries along the equator would not experience seasonal changes.

Name _____   Date _____

Your Kenyan Safari

Imagine you are on your very own Kenyan safari! Research three of the animals you might see on your travels. Write a short description of each animal, along with a few interesting facts, in the boxes below.

◇◇

Animal Name: _____

_____

_____

_____

_____

_____

Animal Name: _____

_____

_____

_____

_____

_____

Animal Name: _____

_____

_____

_____

_____

_____

A History of Kenya

The first humans to enter Kenya are believed to have been the Bantu tribes from West Africa. They came to the land that is now Kenya about a thousand years ago. The coastal regions of the country were dominated by Arabs from the seventh century until explorer Vasco da Gama took possession of Mombasa for Portugal at the end of the 15th century. Around this time, the Nilotic people began to migrate from the north. In 1729, the Portuguese relinquished their power. The Arabs regained control of the coastal regions, which they would maintain until around 1963.

In the 1850s, Europeans became interested in Kenya. They sent explorers in search of the Nile River's source, and missionaries to stop the Arab slave trade and convert the natives to Christianity. By 1855, about 300 missionaries had come to East Africa. This contributed to the end of the slave trade in 1873. In an attempt to colonize Africa, European nations scrambled for a claim in the land. The Anglo-German agreements of 1886 allowed, with the Arab sultan's permission, Germany's East Africa Company to influence the southern coastal region (modern day Tanzania) and Britain's East Africa Company to gain the northern coastal region (modern day Kenya.) At the end of the century, Europeans built railroads through the country. White settlers began arriving in multitudes, driving many native Africans from their homes and claiming much of the land as their own. By 1920, the interior regions of the country were organized into the British colony of Kenya. Britain remained a protectorate of the coastline, but this region was still essentially ruled by the sultan.

Needless to say, the African natives did not like being ruled by the British. This gave rise to constant tension. The British tried to appoint African chiefs and town leaders to enforce their authority, but this did not work well. Through the schools founded by Christian missionaries, educated blacks began to emerge, strongly voicing their desire for independence. They eventually formed the Kenyan African Union (KAU) in 1944. Three years later, a man named Jomo Kenyatta became their leader. During the early 1950s, a terrorist movement called Mau Mau instigated revolts against British authority. Jomo Kenyatta was imprisoned in 1953, but the terrorism and violent revolts continued until 1960.

In 1960, the Kenyan constitution changed from having interracial representation in government to allowing one major political party to run the government. Kenyatta was freed in 1961 and led the Kenyan African National Union to victory in the 1963 elections. Thus, the country became self-governing for the first time. Later that year, Kenya gained full independence, with Kenyatta as the first prime minister. One year later, on December 12, 1964, Kenya became a republic with Kenyatta as the first president.

After its independence, Kenya's economy flourished. The boom lasted until the early 1980s, when it could not combat the rapid growth in population. Poverty and malnutrition spread throughout the country while unemployment was rampant in urban areas. Frustrated with the economic downturn, the people attempted to rise up against the government. In recent years, however, politics in Kenya have improved and it has become a functioning democratic country.

In Your Classroom

Go on a safari of your own. Take the class to a local nature reserve or wildlife oasis. Have them bring notebooks to keep track of the different animals, insects, bugs, birds, and plants they see.

Visit a local zoo, making sure to pay a visit to the lions, elephants, zebras and other animals one might find on a Kenyan safari.

Daily Life

Kenya is filled with diverse groups of people, from those living on the coastal regions, to the urban population, to the pastoral people. As technology develops and communication improves, tribes are disintegrating and much of Kenya's native way of life is disappearing.

Most Kenyan men typically wear shirts with shorts or pants while women wear long dresses known as *khangas*. They do not often wear shoes, and men tend to cover their heads in a skull cap called a *kofia*. Some men wear toga-like outfits called *suka*. Whenever a baby is born, the mother wraps it in cloth and straps it to her back until he or she is old enough to begin walking. Most Africans keep their hair cut short or hide it in a cloth turban. Muslim women cover their heads.

Life in the cities is very similar to western life. Christian Kenyans marry one partner, but polygamy is still present in rural areas. Muslims and tribesman marry with a dowry system—a payment to the bride's family, such as five cows per bride.

Most rural Kenyans are farmers. Families live off the fruit and vegetables they grow on their land, and sell what they don't need at local markets. This is usually the women and children's job. Food is not the only thing being sold at these markets—traders bring handcrafts and other products as well. Money isn't the only currency with which to purchase goods; Kenyans also barter or trade one item for another. Large cities have bigger, more extensive markets than small villages.

Education

There are four distinct levels in the Kenyan education system: early childhood, primary, secondary, and college. Early childhood education takes place from ages three to five, and prepares young students for primary school. Since 2003, the eight years of primary education have been provided to Kenyans for no cost. Upon completing their eighth year, primary students earn the Kenya Certificate of Primary Education, which allows them to move on to four years of secondary. Likewise, a second certificate is earned at the end of secondary, permitting access to colleges and universities.

Religion

Although Kenya has no official religion, many Kenyans consider themselves Christian (45% of which are Protestant and 33% Roman Catholic). There are also a large number of Muslims in the country, as well as Hindus and those who practice indigenous religions. These indigenous religions usually assign divinity to the chief or king, rainfall, or fertility. Many of these tribal religions place faith in a witch doctor to cure disease and protect them from harm. Some League football teams still believe in the witch doctor's power so much that they hire one to place a spell on the ball before a game.

In Your Classroom

Have a market day. Students should bring in a few small things they would like to trade. Spread blankets on the floor and have each student lay out his or her wares. Then let the bartering begin!

Compare an African market to a modern supermarket. What are the similarities and differences?

Famous Kenyan Proverbs

Here are some famous Kenyan proverbs. What do you think they mean?

A donkey always says thank you with a kick.

A sinking ship doesn't need a captain.

All monkeys cannot hang on the same branch.

An empty pot makes the loudest noise.

It is the grass that suffers when elephants fight.

Body Language and Etiquette in Kenya

Here are some examples of body language and etiquette you will find in Kenya.

Kenyans are extremely polite. Always behave in a like fashion. Say please and thank you.

When a younger person greets an elderly person, he or she should show respect by bowing to the elder.

Do not shake hands or give gifts with your left hand – this is considered rude.

It is extremely rude to point at someone or beckon them over with your index finger.

During conversation, avoid excessive direct eye contact. Too much is considered impolite.

Swahili

Swahili is the official language of Kenya. Grammatically it is a Bantu language and is heavily influenced by Arabic, although written with Roman letters. English is the other official language and is widely spoken. In the highland regions, people often speak Bantu and Nilo-Himatic languages in numerous dialects, depending on their ethnic group.

Swahili is easy to pronounce because each letter is sounded out. Here are some useful words and phrases:

English	Swahili
Hello.	Jambo / hujambo / Salama
How are you?	Habari gani?
Fine (response)	Nzuri
See you later.	Tutaonana.
Nice to meet you.	Nafurahi kukuona.
Goodnight	Lala salama
Yes	Ndiyo
No	Hapana
Thank you.	Asante.
Please	Tafadhali
OK	Sawa
Excuse me.	Samahani.
You're welcome.	Starehe.
What is your name?	Jina lako nani?
My name is…	Jina langu ni …
Where are you from?	Unatoka wapi?
I'm from …	Natokea …
Do you speak English?	Unasema kiingereza?
Do you speak Swahili?	Unasema Kiswahili?
Just a little bit	Kidogo tu
I don't understand.	Sielewi.
Friend	Rafiki

Numbers

1	moja
2	mbili
3	tatu
4	nne
5	tano
6	sita
7	saba
8	nane
9	tisa
10	kumi
11	kumi na moja (ten and one)
12	kumi na mbili (ten and two)

In Your Classroom

For one day, use Swahili numbers instead of English ones.

42

Speaking of Swahili...

Use the Swahili translations on page 42 to write a short dialogue between two Kenyans meeting for the first time. Give each character a Kenyan name, too!

◇◇

Character 1: _____

Character 2: _____

_____

_____

_____

_____

_____

_____

_____

_____

_____

_____

_____

_____

_____

_____

FOODS

Kenya's cuisine is a combination of the country's resources and historical influences. The varied regions of the land provide a variety of sustenance, and the long history of foreign presence has contributed many elements. The resulting fare is distinctive and delicious.

The climate and terrain of Kenya allow for a wide variety of crops to grow and flourish. This is especially true of the country's fruit. Some of the fruits available are mangoes, watermelons, oranges, papaya, pineapples, bananas, guavas, passion fruit, and coconuts.

Passion fruit

Early Kenyan peoples practiced cattle herding, and came to appreciate all that these creatures can provide. They used the cattle for milk, butter, and meat. They even incorporated a cow's blood into their diets! This tradition is evident in modern tribes like the *Maasai*, a cattle- and goat-herding society. They depend upon these animals for their food, and their common meals and dishes reflect that reliance.

European involvement in the region had an enormous impact on Kenyan food. The Portuguese introduced many crops that are now staples in the national diet. Examples include maize, bananas, peppers, sweet potatoes, and pork, among other fruits, vegetables, and livestock. Other Europeans brought potatoes, tomatoes, and cucumbers. Their Indian slaves brought more exotic foods to Kenyan shores: curries, chapattis (bread), and chutneys among them. The eastern coast was deeply affected by the Arab influence, along with other traders and visitors. These diverse elements have fused with Kenyan tradition and crops to create modern Kenyan cuisine.

Some Kenyan Dishes

Irio is a common meal made from corn, beans, potatoes, and various greens. The ingredients are mashed together and rolled into balls. These balls are dipped in different stews to add taste.

One of the national dishes of Kenya is *Ugali*, a thick maize-based porridge eaten across the country nearly every day. It is often eaten with a meat or some form of stew. Sometimes, ugali is mixed with something called *sukuma wiki*. This is spinach or other green vegetables fried together with onions, tomatoes, peppers, and meat.

Nyama choma is the second national dish of Kenya. It is roasted or grilled goat served with mashed vegetables. The meat is cooked with very little seasoning and is served in bite-size chunks.

Kachumbari is a mixture of chopped tomatoes, onions, pepper, cilantro, lemon juice, and avocado. It is served with nyama choma and ugali.

A great example of an eastern shore meal is *wali*. This is simply rice boiled in coconut milk. It is specifically a coastal dish because of the coconut trees that grow along the shore.

Looking for something that will satisfy a sweet tooth? Try *maandazi*, deep-fried sweets very similar to doughnuts. These are often eaten at breakfast, along with hot tea or coffee, but that doesn't stop Kenyans from snacking on them in the afternoon!

44

Holidays & Festivals

Here are some of the public holidays and festivals celebrated in Kenya.

Madaraka Day
June 1

On this day in 1963, Jomo Kenyatta became prime minister of Kenya. This was symbolic of Kenyan self-government, and signaled the coming of full independence. Kenyans remember their struggle to be free, and the heroic figures that contributed to that freedom.

Mashujaa Day (Heroes' Day)
October 20

Formerly Kenyatta Day, in recognition of Jomo Kenyatta, Kenya's first president and a prominent figure in the independence movement, Heroes' Day was declared in 2010. The day is marked by a presidential speech and a military parade through Nairobi and other areas.

Obama Day
November 6

A new holiday (as of 2009), this national celebration commemorates the election of Barack Obama as president of the United States of America. Why is this event celebrated in Kenya, you ask? Obama's father was born in Kenya.

Jamhuri Day
December 12

The Swahili word for *republic*, Jamhuri Day celebrates December 12, 1964, the day Kenya became a republic. Many festivals are held to recognize the country's rich culture and history. This is considered the most important holiday of the year. Kenyans wear brightly clothes in the nation's colors, and proudly hang the country's flag. Traditional Kenyan food is enjoyed with family and friends.

Other common public holidays celebrated in Kenya include New Year's Day, Good Friday, Easter Monday, Labour Day, Eid al-Fitr (End of Ramadan), Christmas Day, and Boxing Day.

Creative Arts

Literature

Oral traditions of the native Kenyans heavily influenced their modern written literature. Ancient histories have been passed down from generation to generation through the oral tradition. Drums and other instruments and dancing often accompany these retellings. Contemporary authors who have been influenced by the ancient traditions are: James Ngugi Wa Thoingo, Muga Gicaru, and Josiah Kariuki. Wa Thoingo's book *Weep Not, Child* describes life in Kenya during Britain's rule. In his story, he writes about the effects the Mau Mau movement had on the lives of black Kenyans. It has become one of the best-known novels in African literature. M.G. Vassanji's novel *In-Between World of Vikram Lall* won the Giller Prize in 2003. This novel is a fictional memoir of adjusting to the political changes of colonial and post-colonial Kenya.

Music

Many of the tribal peoples of Kenya practice traditional and specific forms of music. The Maasai sing chants. The Akamba specialize in percussion instruments and music. The Gusii play instruments called obokano, which are large pipes similar to lutes. These, along with many other traditional styles and instruments, have been passed down through generations. They are a very important part of Kenyan culture.

Modern music involves much use of the guitar, the most common popular instrument. Fundi Konde, a well-known and talented guitarist, was instrumental in popularizing the guitar. He also helped spread the music around Kenya with his work in radio broadcasting.

Today, Kenyan young people listen to all kinds of music from around the world: pop, rock and roll, hip hop, and reggae are just a few of the more popular genres.

Arts and Crafts

Kenyans are known for their handcraft. Wood carvings and soapstone carvings are common forms of Kenyan artwork, particularly as done by the Kamba people. Nairobi is the center for national art and is home to the National Museum, the Kenya Cultural Center, and the National Theater.

In Your Classroom

Find a traditional Kenyan poem and read it aloud. Ask students what the poem means, and how it makes them feel. Have children write their own poems as inspired by the material read.

# Sports & Games

Kenyans compete in a number of sports. Cricket, soccer, rugby, rallying, and boxing are the most popular, but the country is especially well-known for its dominance in distance and middle-distance running. Kenya's most famous athletes include: Catherine Ndereba, four-time women's Boston Marathon winner and two-time world champion, and Paul Tergat, former Marathon world-record holder.

Another sport being taken over by Kenyans is women's volleyball. Various club and national teams have won several international tournaments and competitions in recent years.

Since 1996, Kenya has competed in the Cricket World Cup. It is also an important competitor in the rugby union and in FIFA (International Federation of Association Football). Rallying is very popular, especially the Safari Rally which draws drivers from all over the world because of its reputation as one of the toughest rallies in the world.

Kenya performed very well in the 2008 Summer Olympics in Beijing, China. Kenyan athletes won five gold medals, five silver medals, and four bronze medals, for a total of 14, making it the most successful African country at the Games.

Madagascar

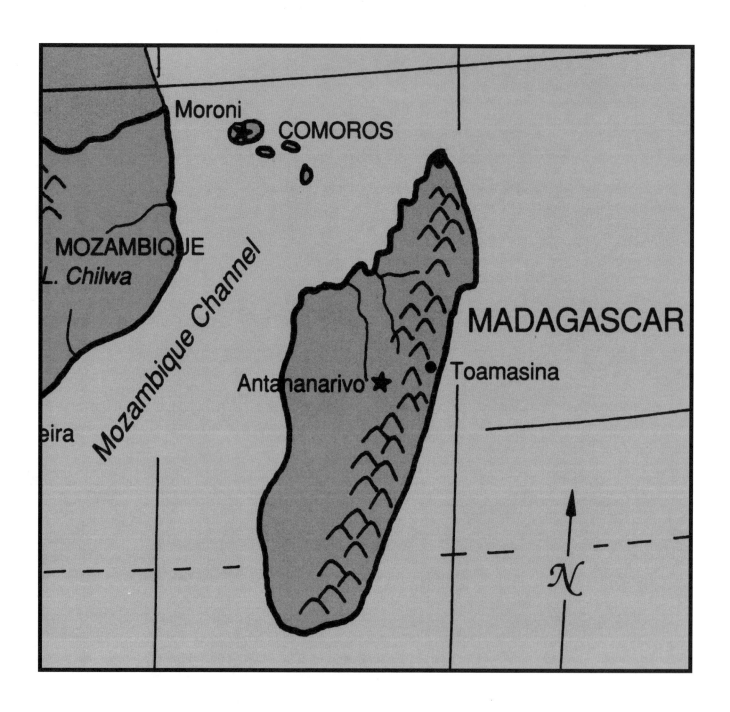

Welcome to Madagascar!

Madagascar, the fourth largest island in the world, is located across the Mozambique Channel from the southeastern coast of Africa. This island nation, approximately the size of Texas, is situated in the Indian Ocean, and has remained relatively isolated from the rest of Africa.

FAST FACTS

Official name: Republic of Madagascar

Location: This island nation is found in the Indian Ocean, off the southeast coast of the main African continent.

Population: 21,926,221 (2010 estimate)

Capital City: Antananarivo

Area: 226,597 square miles

Major Languages: French and Malagasy are both official languages.

Major Religions: Indigenous beliefs: 52%
Christianity: 41%
Muslim: 7%

Currency: Malagasy *ariary*

Climate: Madagascar features three distinct climates: tropical along the coast, temperate inland, and arid to the south.

The Land: Mountains and high plateaus are surrounded by narrow coastal plains.

Type of Government: Republic

Flag: The flag of Madagascar is comprised of three colors—one vertical white stripe alongside two horizontal stripes, one red and another green. The colors of the Madagascan flag represent the country's longing for independence and traditional classes. Red and white were the colors in the flag of Ranavalona III, the last queen of the *Merina* kingdom, which was overtaken by France at the end of the 19th century. These colors are the same as those in the flag of Indonesia and perhaps indicate a shared heritage with Southeast Asia. Green was the color of the *Hova*, a group of peasants who played an important role in the anti-French movement which led to the island's independence.

National Seal:	The circular seal features an outline of the island at its center, with green and red rays shining from the island, creating an image of the sun. The head of a *Zebu* (cattle) is positioned beneath the outline. Other colors present on the seal are yellow, black, and white.
National Animal:	Ring Tailed Lemur
National Motto:	*"Tanindrazana, Fahafahana, Fandrosoana"* (Malagasy for *"Ancestral-land, Liberty, Progress"*)

Natural Environment

Madagascar is known for its hills, gorges, volcanic remains, and its central plateau—a high upland region in the center of the island. The country's average elevation is about 4,500 feet. The tallest peak, Mount Maromokotro, has an elevation of 9,436 feet. Most people on the island live in the central plateau, which is where the capital city of Antananarivo is located. The most densely populated area is a 30 mile-wide plain located between the plateau and the Indian Ocean. Toamasina, Madagascar's leading port, is located there.

The sparsely populated west is home to savanna-like plains and fertile valleys surrounding the rivers Betisboka, Tsiri-bihina, and Mangoky, which descend from the plateau to the coast of the Mozambique Channel. Next to the east coast of the island are The Canal des Pangalenes. This chain of natural and man-made lakes is connected by canals and runs beside the coast for nearly two-thirds of the island.

Madagascar is often referred to as the "Red Island" because of the color of its soil, which has been exposed by erosion. Bamboo and savanna-like grass grow throughout the island. Unfortunately, the plateau has suffered from deforestation, which is endangering some animal species. To combat this, a reforestation program has begun through the planting of pines and eucalyptus to replenish the tree population and alleviate severe soil erosion.

Ring-Tailed Lemur

The remaining forests house a large variety of unique animals and plant life, many found nowhere else in the world. In fact, Madagascar has been referred to as "the eighth continent" because of this fact. Madagascar is home to half of the world's chameleon varieties, most surviving lemurs, baobab trees and more than 6,000 species of flowers. Cattle, a traditional symbol of wealth, were once used in religious practices. They continue to roam the island in large numbers. The island is also home to many rocks and minerals, some of which are mined (chromium, salt, graphite, mica, beryl, zircon, gold, and garnets among them).

Weather is unpredictable, as the island experiences irregular rainfall throughout the year. Severe cyclones usually strike Madagascar several times each year. The east and southeast experience the greatest precipitation, the west and southwest the least. The central plateau is the coolest part of the island due to its elevation, and receives about 53 inches of rainfall each year.

Madagascar's economy is based almost solely on its agriculture, with rice, cassava, coffee, cloves and vanilla as its major crops. It is the world's leading vanilla producer. Despite this, the country suffers from poverty. The island relies on foreign aid from the United States, France, and other western European countries. Madagascar's most important industries are food processing and textile manufacturing.

In Your Classroom

Using construction paper, poster board, and paint, create your own Madagascar flag to hang in the classroom. Discuss what each color in the flag represents.

Make a map of Madagascar, labeling the major cities and rivers. Make sure the map is large enough so it is visible to the entire classroom.

Discuss the problem of deforestation. What are the causes? What are the effects? Determine creative ways your classroom can preserve paper (and therefore trees.) These could include always using both sides of a piece of paper, having oral quizzes rather than written ones, bringing lunch in plastic containers rather than bags and boxes, and recycling.

Avoid deforestation in your area. Begin a garden in the classroom (pea or bean plants work best) and replant the plants outside once they are too big for their pots.

Learn About Lemurs

The national animal of Madagascar is the Ring-Tailed Lemur. These creatures are cute and fascinating! Research these interesting beasts. Write a two or three paragraph summary of what you learn. Study their habitat, the foods they eat, how they work together as a group, and other characteristics. Find a picture of a ring-tailed lemur and paste it to this page.

◇◇◇

_____

_____

_____

_____

_____

_____

_____

_____

_____

_____   *Paste picture here*

_____

_____

_____

A History of Madagascar

During the first century CE, Indonesian seafarers arrived in Madagascar from the coast of East Africa and Southeast Asia. Arab traders also began to visit the island to set up trading posts along the coast. Madagascar soon developed into a key port connecting trade routes between Africa and Asia. In 1500, a Portuguese navigator named Diogo Dias became the first European to arrive on the island. He was followed by the French, who set up a trading post at Fort Dauphin in 1642. From the end of the 16th century to the beginning of the 17th, Madagascar was a favorite haunt for pirates, and many sailors were shipwrecked on the island.

The Merina dynasty came to power in the late 16th century and ruled the country for about 300 years. The Merina kingdom founded its capital at Antananarivo and continued to control the island until the end of the 19th century. While the Merinas were in power, the island population was made up of three different social classes: the *andriana* (aristocracy), *hova* (common people), and *andevo* (slaves). During the latter half of Merina rule, Europeans continued to arrive on the island. In 1895, Madagascar became a French colony.

After the French annexed Madagascar, the country experienced a surge of improvements and sophistications. The capital was upgraded with wide paved roads and museums. Schools were constructed, and education became mandatory for those aged six to 13. Plantations were created in order to export crops and a system of railways and roads were designed to connect the rest of the island to Antananarivo.

During World War II, Madagascar was occupied by British and South African Forces. In 1943, it was turned over to the Free French, which led to a revolt in 1947. This revolt was violently suppressed, causing between as many as 80,000 deaths. In 1960, what was formerly known as the Malagasy Republic became an independent nation under President Philibert Tsiranana; however, violent riots later forced Tsiranana to turn over his power to General Gabriel Ranamantsoa. In 1975, after years of turmoil, Didier Ratsiraka became president. The new government established a constitution that changed the country's name to the Democratic Republic of Madagascar. This constitution provided for a president to be elected every seven years. Ratsiraka was reelected in 1982 and again in 1989.

In recent years, Madagascar has suffered internal conflicts due to controversial election results. In 2009, a new government was established by military force. Because of its corrupt beginnings, this new government is not recognized by several international entities, including the European Union and the African Union. As of today, the political situation in Madagascar is still in transition, and the ultimate future of this beautiful and wild country is uncertain.

Daily Life

Population and Regions

The majority of people living in Madagascar are of Malayo-Polynesian (Southeast Asian/Pacific Islander) origin, but have intermixed with the Arab and African populations as well. The Malagasy are divided into 18 different ethnic groups whose conflicts between each other cause constant problems. The *Merina* are the largest of these groups and are predominately Indonesian in origin. The Merina live on the plateau along with the *Betsileo* people. Other major tribes include: the *Betsimisaraka* in the east, the *Antandroy* in the south, the *Tsimihety* in the north, and the coastal people called *côtiers*. The vast majority of the population is Malagasy, but small minorities from the Comoros, France, India and China are also present.

Religion

About 50 percent of the population practice traditional religions which center on ancestor worship. Madagascans have a great deal of respect for the dead. 45 percent of the population is Christian, with that number being equally divided between Catholics and Protestants. The remaining percentage of the population practice Islam.

Houses

Different regions of the country feature different architectural styles. These styles are largely dependent upon the materials the land makes available for construction. In the central highlands, near the capital of Antananarivo, many homes and buildings are two-story stone structures. As you travel further out from the interior, you will see more plant material constructions. Houses are usually four-sided structures with peaked roofing.

Village in Madagascar

Education

Children between the ages of six and 14 are required to attend school. The Madagascan system is divided into two parts – primary and secondary. Primary lasts between the ages of six and 11. Secondary is broken into two subdivisions – junior and senior – that take place from age 12 to age 18. Certificates are earned, allowing entry into the next higher level. Higher education exists in the University of Madagascar, a six-branch college spread across the island. The school is very crowded with thousands more students than capacity, and very few students complete the long programs offered.

The condition of education in Madagascar is very poor. A traditionally sound system that began experiencing difficulties several years ago, the country's education system was dealt a severe blow by the political crisis of 2009. Due to the unstable state of the nation, foreign aid has been virtually cut off. This has further complicated a wide variety of problems facing Madagascan education reform. Poor teacher quality, material shortages, lack of access to secondary schools, poverty, and poor student health are just some of the issues affecting the children of Madagascar.

In Your Classroom

Break the students into several small groups. Have each group develop a tribe. They should choose a tribe name, location, and several tribal characteristics.

Take students outside and have them collect a variety of plant materials – leaves, twigs, blades of grass, etc. Build a model Madagascan house.

Discuss the problems affecting education in Madagascar. Ask students for ideas for improving the situation. Have them compare their lives at school to those of Madagascan students.

Famous Madagascan Proverbs

Here are some famous Madagascan proverbs. What do you think they mean?

Distracted by what is far away, he does not see his nose.

It is better to refuse than to accept and not to go.

Words are like eggs. When they are hatched, they have wings.

Body Language and Etiquette in Madagascar

Here are some examples of body language and etiquette you will find in Madagascar.

Conservative clothing is the preferred style of dress in Madagascar.

Being late is unacceptable in Madagascar. Try to always be on time.

When you are a guest in another's home, you should bring a small gift to show your appreciation.

The Malagasy Language

Malagasy and French are the official languages of Madagascar. The Malagasy language originated from the Malayo-Polynesian language and borrows from French and Arabic, as well as the Bantu languages of southern Africa. In recent years, the government has promoted teaching English in numerous primary schools throughout the country, hoping to make it part of the nationwide educational curriculum.

Here are some Malagasy translations for common English words and phrases.

English	Malagasy
Yes	Eny
No	Tsia
Hello.	Salama.
Goodbye.	Veloma.
Please	Azafady
Thank you.	Misaotra.
What's your name?	Iza no anaranao?

Numbers

one	isa
two	roa
three	telo
four	efatra
five	dimy
six	enina
seven	fito
eight	valo
nine	sivy
ten	folo

FOODS

Madagascans eat their dinners from mats on the floor. In cities, however, they eat off plates and use a large spoon. Their food is not very spicy, but it is flavorful. They are fond of fresh fruits and vegetables. A meal often starts with vegetable soup and more vegetables are served with the entrée. Chicken or fish curry are popular entrees, and rice is served at each meal. In fact, Madagascar has the world's highest consumption of rice per capita. Along with their meal, Madagascans have a drink called *ranonapango*, which is made by burning rice and then adding water to it. After the meal, they usually eat fresh fruit flavored with vanilla as a dessert.

Laoka

Laoka is the Malagasy word for accompaniment, those food items that are served alongside the ever-present rice. Laoka are prepared and served in a number of different and unique ways. They are often presented in sauces, from tomato to coconut to milk. Some ingredient combinations include: peas and pork, beef, or fish; shredded cassava leaves with peanuts, beef, or pork; beef or chicken with ginger or garlic; and various types of seafood. A condiment called *sakay*, made from red or green chili pepper, is often added.

56

Food on the Go

If you're walking around a Madagascan city or village and hunger strikes, don't worry. There are a variety of street foods that will keep you moving. Malagasy Bread is a cooked batter of sweetened rice flour. *Mofo gasy*, made from coconut milk, is a sweet snack often served with coffee. Other sweets include deep-fried doughnuts and fruit fritters.

Koba akondro is made of ground peanuts, mashed bananas, honey, and corn flour. All of this is placed in a bed of banana leaves and steamed until the batter sets.

Other vendors will sell you tasty peanut brittle, dried bananas, deep-fried dough, yogurt, and steamed sweet potatoes.

Desserts

Madagascans don't ignore their tastes for the sweeter things in life. The country is known for its delicious cocoa and vanilla, but there are other desserts to choose from. Fresh fruits are a common item, usually sprinkled with sugar or vanilla. These include apples, lemons, pumpkins, watermelons, strawberries, oranges, and cherries. *Koba* is made by grinding peanuts and brown sugar. This is mixed with sweetened rice flour paste and put inside banana leaves and boiled for two days. Another Madagascan specialty is *Bonbon coco*, balls of shredded coconut and caramelized sugar. French involvement in Madagascar's history is obvious in the country's love for pastries and cakes.

Holidays & Festivals

Here are some public holidays celebrated in Madagascar.

New Year's Day • *January 1*

Martyrs' Day • *March 29* • commemorates the 1947 rebellion and those that gave their lives

Easter Monday • *date varies*

Labour Day • *May 1* • celebrates Madagascar's workers

Ascension • *date varies* • celebrates the ascension of Jesus Christ

Whit Monday • *date varies* • celebrates baptisms that took place after the Christian festival of Pentecost

Independence Day • *June 26* • celebrates the day Madagascar earned their independence

Assumption • *August 15* • celebrates the ascension of Mary, mother of Jesus Christ

All Saints Day • *November 1*

Christmas Day • *December 25*

Creative Arts

Music

Madagascan music can be divided into three separate styles: traditional, contemporary, and popular. Traditional music is dependent upon region and history. The *valiha*, a tube zither (stringed instrument) made from bamboo, is played in the central highlands, often joined by singers. The valiha is considered the national instrument of Madagascar. In the south, singing styles from South Africa, along with instruments like the piano and acoustic guitar, are common.

Contemporary music involves traditional styles mixed with more modern developments, including the electric guitar, bass guitar, and drums. Synthesizers are also added. Modern genres from all over the world, like rock and roll, gospel, jazz, reggae, and hip hop have all joined the Madagascan sound. Popular music holds the sounds of both traditional and contemporary music taken in bold new directions.

The Importance of Stories

Madagascar has a rich tradition of oral history and storytelling. Many of the stories and myths of the Madagascan people have been woven into an epic poem titled the *Ibonia*. It exists in many forms around the island, each unique to different peoples, places, and histories.

Valiha

There are many supernatural elements, such as magic, witches, and multiple gods and ancestors, in the stories and poems of the Malagasy. These tales are not mere stories, however. They communicate the history and traditions of the Malagasy peoples from generation to generation, preserving the island's rich past.

Arts and Crafts

There are many forms of art and craft practiced around Madagascar. Textile art is one example. Hand-woven clothes known as *lamba* are given as gifts and symbolize the creator's cultural heritage. These fabrics are often bright and beautiful.

Some ancient funerary art has survived the passage of time. Sculptures and monuments were created for the deceased. Figures of birds, called *mijoa*, are very common. They symbolize the connection between life and death, and are sometimes represented in pairs.

There are many other forms of Madagascan art, including fantasy and poster art, as well as impressionist and modern art. As the country continues to discover a national identity, more diverse forms emerge on the global art scene.

Sports & Games

Popular sports in Madagascar include tennis, basketball, football, track and field, boxing, and judo. *Maraingy*, or hand-to-hand combat, is a very popular spectator sport practiced by both men and women. In some regions, Madagascans wrestle zebu, or cows!

The country's national teams are the Davis Cup and Federation Cup tennis teams, representing the country internationally. Two sisters, Dally and Natacha Randriantefy, have competed in tennis at the US Open and the Olympic Games.

Nature lovers and outdoor sports enthusiasts flock to Madagascar's 2,500 mile coastline. Its coral reefs, beaches, sandbars and marine life attract tourists and natives alike.

Beach near Fort Dauphin, Madagascar

Nigeria

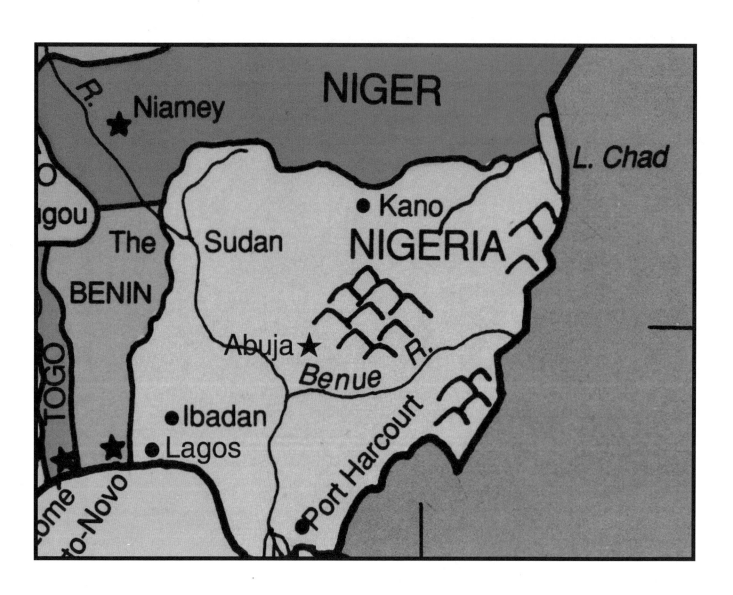

Welcome to Nigeria!

FAST FACTS

Official name: Federal Republic of Nigeria

Location: Located between Benin and Cameroon, Nigeria is in Western Africa. Niger borders to the north, with the Gulf of Guinea to the south.

Population: 155,215,573 (2010 estimate)

Capital City: Abuja

Area: 356,667 square miles

Major Language: English

Major Religions: Muslim: 50%
Christian: 40%
Indigenous beliefs: 10%

Currency: Nigerian *naira*

Climate: The north experiences an arid climate; the center has a tropical climate; and the south has an equatorial climate.

The Land: Lowlands and mountains make up the south, with central plateaus and hills in the center. The north is dominated by plains.

Type of Government: Federal Republic

Flag: Three equal vertical stripes of green, white, and green make up the Nigerian flag. The green stripes represent the forests and natural resources of the country. The white stripe symbolizes peace and unity.

Coat of Arms: The Nigerian coat of arms features a black shield with two white banners joining upon it to form a Y formation. The white banners are the two rivers flowing through the country, and the black of the shield is the good earth. An eagle sits atop the shield, symbolizing strength. Two horses flank the shield, representing dignity.

National Flower: Costus Spectabilis (Spiral Ginger)

National Motto: "Unity and Faith, Peace and Progress"

Natural Environment

Nigeria is a country in West Africa, located on the Gulf of Guinea, part of the Atlantic Ocean. The country is bordered by Niger in the north, the Republic of Benin in the west, and Chad and Cameroon to the east. The country's landscape varies, with rainforests, mountains, savannas, beaches and desert. Nigeria's highest peak is Chappal Waddi. It reaches an elevation of 7,936 feet. Its main rivers, the Niger and the Benue, join together and empty into the largest river delta in the world—the Niger Delta. This region is home to a large oil industry and experiences numerous environmental problems, such as oil spills, deforestation, and waste management and sewage treatment problems.

The climate varies by region, with the south experiencing a tropical rainforest climate. The north has desert-like conditions, and the area in between is a moderate savanna—a grassland ecosystem with trees and occasional patches of sand. The forests of Nigeria consist of mangrove and fresh water swamps, and are home to diverse wildlife. The drill monkey, distinct to southeastern Nigeria and Cameroon, is found in the wild in this area. This region is also home to the world's largest diversity of butterflies.

In Your Classroom

Research and discuss the environmental problems Nigeria faces. How could the government combat these? How do these problems effect global warming/climate change? What similar problems does your region have? How can you change things in your own country?

Assign one student per day to be the "waste manager." This person is in charge of making sure there is no litter left in the classroom. He or she must enforce rules so other students keep the classroom tidy, but at the end of the day he or she is responsible for the state of the room.

A HISTORY OF NIGERIA

Nigeria has an extensive history dating back to 9000 BCE. Archeologists have discovered ancient smelting furnaces near Taruga. These furnaces were used around 4 BCE, and are the oldest evidence of metalworking to this date. Archeologists have also unearthed terracotta sculptures created by the Nok people, the first to develop Nigerian culture. These people lived on the Jos Plateau in northeastern Nigeria, and by 200 CE had established an active trade route through the Sahara to North Africa.

Today, Nigeria is divided into 36 states of different ethnic groups. Throughout its history, some of the important early states included: Yoruba kingdoms, the Edo kingdom of Benin, the Igbo kingdom of Nri, Hausa cities, and the Calabar kingdoms. The kingdom of Nri was the oldest state of Nigeria and is considered to be the cradle of Nigerian civilization. This kingdom existed from 900 CE and lasted over a thousand years. Other states existed but were either absorbed by larger ethnic groups, or no archeological evidence remains from them today.

The various kingdoms of Nigeria have different customs and traditions. The Yoruba kingdoms were diverse and comprised of migrants from the Arabian Peninsula who formed their own clans and followed their own chiefs. These clans settled on the western bank of the Niger River. As their cities developed, so did their art—particularly their metal castings and terracotta and ivory sculptures. The Yoruba believed in many gods, with Olorun as the head god and Oduduwa, the ancestor of Yoruba kings, as the creator god.

The Igbo kingdoms began to emerge and establish themselves after the Nri kingdom's decline in 1400-1600 CE. Like the Yoruba, the Igbo people believed in many gods, with one central god, Ala, representing mother earth and fertility. The city of Nri is known as the foundation of Igbo culture. Eri, the god-like founder of Nri culture, is believed to have settled the area around 948. But archeologists have uncovered royal burials from at least 900 CE or earlier.

The kingdoms of Oyo and Benin became centers for economic and political power during the 15th century. They established important trade routes, reaching as far as Portugal. Hausa states were known for their walled towns, trading, manufacturing, and caravans. Other tribes began to infiltrate the Hausa region, introducing animal herding to the people. Islam began to arrive in Hausa through the caravan routes and began to shape the culture.

The Efík kingdom, also known as the Calabar, was active in ancient trading. It was the first kingdom on record to use money in West Africa trading. The society was ruled by kings, but after it became a British colony in 1901, the title was changed to *Obong*, so as not to be confused with the British monarchy. The city of Calabar became the first Nigerian capital, but when Nigeria gained its independence in 1960, the city was divided with half of it belonging to Cameroon.

In 1963, Nigeria declared itself to be a Federal Republic, making its former governor, Nnamdi Azikiwe, its first president. Nigeria faced many problems between its ethnic groups, both religious and economic. The people in the north were educated very differently from those in the south, and tension arose. Three different political parties with different religious views from the Yoruba, Hausa, and Igbo regions formed. After numerous disputes and riots during the 1965 elections, a group of southeastern Igbo army officers assassinated the prime minister and overthrew the government. The federal military attempted to rule the country, but the ethnic and religious tensions soon grew out of hand and the military leadership was overthrown. This led to the Nigerian Civil War, in which an estimated one million people were killed. After the war, random fighting continued until the late 1970s, when a new government was established and a new constitution was published. Again, the military overthrew the government and replaced its leaders with military rulers.

Eventually, the country established a new government with two political parties: the National Republic Convention and the Social Democratic Party. In 1993, Nigeria returned to civilian rule; however, the presidential elections were initially annulled and peace was not established until 1999. The new government had much to deal with: dysfunctional bureaucracy, political and religious turmoil, a powerful military resistance, economic problems, and human rights violations. Although conditions are improving in Nigeria, the country still experiences political and religious turmoil, tension over environmental destruction due to oil drilling in the Niger delta, military unrest, violence, and electoral fraud.

Daily Life

Family

Families are the central institution of Nigerian culture. Weddings and births are celebrated by large gatherings and families congregate together for funerals as well. To celebrate happy events (such as weddings, births, and adult-hood), families and communities join together in performing special dances to show their support for one another. Masks and other decorations are used in traditional dancing. Home entertainment such as radio, television, movies, and music are popular ways for the family to pass time together, particularly in urban homes.

Cities and Villages

Nigeria's population is comprised of over 250 ethnic groups with varying languages and customs. The largest of these groups, the Fulani/Hausa, Yoruba, and Igbo, make up 68 percent of the population. A small amount of minorities from other countries have migrated to Nigeria, including ex-slaves who won their emancipation in Latin America.

The cities of Nigeria suffer from excessive pollution and waste management problems due to poor industrial planning, as well as growing population and poverty issues. Nigeria is heavily involved with US trading and supplies one-fifth of America's oil supply. In turn, Nigeria exports many US products. Petroleum is Nigeria's largest industry and main export, but its telecommunications market, financial services, mineral resources, agriculture, and manufacturing also play a large role in its economy.

Clothing

Because there are so many ethnic groups in Nigeria, many of them have their own clothing and sense of style. The people in the north tend to be more practical in their dress, wearing what is appropriate for their work. In the south, people are fonder of dressing up.

Nigerian clothing is colorful and made from materials such as lace, jacquard, adire, and Ankara. Women wear a *kaba*, a single piece dress which comes in a variety of styles. Over this they wear a *buba*, a loose blouse that comes below the waist. They wrap an *Iro*, which is a rectangular piece of cloth, around the waist. For head gear, they tie a piece of cloth called a *gele* around their head. Sometimes they wear a *borun* or *ipele*—a scarf tied across the body or around the neck. Nigerian men also wear *bubas* that go halfway down the thighs. Men also wear caps called *filas* and pants called *sokotos*. With varieties of colors and fabrics, Nigerian dress can be quite creative.

Education

The educational system in Nigeria is lacking; only 68 percent of the population can read and write. Education is free, but not mandatory, and consists of six years of primary school, three years of junior secondary school, and three years of senior secondary school. Only 30 percent of the population attends secondary school. For those who complete secondary education and wish to further their studies, four years of university education is available. In 2004, the Nigerian National Planning Commission called the country's education system "dysfunctional."

64

Beliefs and Practices

The main religions in Nigeria are Islam, Christianity, indigenous religions, and minority spiritual groups such as Hinduism, Judaism, Baháí Faith, along with a combination of Christianity and Islam known as "Chrislam." Most Nigerian Muslims are Sunni and reside in the northern part of the country. The Christian population is almost evenly divided between Catholics and Protestants who reside in the southern part of the country. In an area known as *Yarubaland*, which comprises western Nigeria, Benin, and Togo, people tend to follow a religion that teaches their divine destiny is to achieve *Orisha*, or to become one with God.

The Nri people believed in *taboos*—superstitions that specific things and events were evil. Some of these taboos were the birth of twins, killing or eating pythons, and certain behaviors, objects, and types of speech. Their religion required that they abide by the rules of taboo and obey their god-king, the *Eze Nri*.

Social Issues

Many Nigerians suffer from poor health due to an unclean environment and faulty health system. Polio, cholera, and malaria are common diseases. Fortunately, Nigeria has a lower number of people with AIDS/HIV than other African countries. But because of the lack of sanitation, life expectancy is very low.

Human rights issues pervade the country. Violence and abuses are common occurrences among the people of Nigeria. In recent years, the government has been making improvements, but the country still has a long way to go.

In Your Classroom

Discuss various family traditions the students have, and traditions in general. Are weddings and births family affairs like they are in Nigeria? Do students think the family is central to their social structure? What do they do with their families as pastimes?

Make masks like many Nigerians do for special occasions. Use paper plates, paper bags, construction paper, or cardboard. Decorate the masks with colorful paints, bright paper, or glitter.

Discuss taboos in today's culture. These could be superstitions such as crossing paths with a black cat, breaking a mirror, or walking under a ladder. Have the students share their opinions about taboos. Do they believe in them? Do they think certain objects or situations are unlucky? Why or why not?

Contrast taboos with good luck charms, such as four-leaf clovers and horseshoes. Assign students to research these objects and discover how they became known as "lucky charms." What are symbols of luck in other cultures?

Language & Expressions

An estimated 521 languages are spoken throughout Nigeria. English was chosen as the official language of Nigeria with the hopes that it would unite the different cultures and languages of the country. Since Nigeria had been a British country, English seemed the best choice; however, while it is used in education, business and for official purposes, it is not spoken in rural areas.

Nigeria's main languages represent three major families of African languages: Niger-Congo (such as Yoruba and Igbo), Hausal (Afro-Asiatic), and Kanuri, primarily spoken in the northeast state of Borno (Nilo-Saharan). Pidgin English, a mixture of indigenous languages and broken English, is also widely spoken.

Famous Nigerian Proverbs

Here are some famous Nigerian proverbs. What do you think they mean?

A man who is trampled to death by an elephant is a man who is blind and deaf.

It is little by little that a bird builds its nest.

However long the moon disappears, someday it must shine again.

A single tree cannot make a forest.

He who digs a pit for others must invariably fall in it.

Body Language and Etiquette in Nigeria

Here are some examples of body language and etiquette you will find in Nigeria.

When you meet someone, be sure to smile. This is very important in Nigeria.

Don't use someone's first name until you are invited to.

When meeting an elder, respect and deference should be shown with a bow of the head.

Give gifts with either the right hand or both hands simultaneously. Giving gifts with the left hand is very inappropriate.

Close friends and family members will hug and kiss when they meet each other.

66

Write a New Language

Did you know that more than 500 languages are spoken in Nigeria? It's your turn to write your own language. Create translations for the words listed below. Write the new words on the lines provided. Then choose ten more words and write translations. Practice your new language with friends!

◇◇◇◇◇◇◇◇◇◇◇◇◇◇◇◇◇◇◇◇◇◇◇◇◇◇◇◇◇◇◇◇◇◇◇◇◇◇

Hello _____   Goodbye _____

Thanks _____   Yes _____

No _____   Friend _____

Family _____   Home _____

School _____   Book _____

Pencil _____   Paper _____

Bicycle _____   Automobile _____

Tree _____   River _____

Hands _____   Hair _____

Shoes _____   Shirt _____

New words   **Translations**

_____   _____

_____   _____

_____   _____

_____   _____

_____   _____

_____   _____

_____   _____

_____   _____

_____   _____

_____   _____

FOODS

Like most West African cuisine, Nigerian food is known for its different flavorings and variety. Seafood, beef, goat, and chicken are popular dishes. Herbs, spices, oils, and chili peppers are used to make delicious, spicy sauces. In the south, vegetable-based soups are popular. Rice, beans, and root vegetables are eaten all over the country, and northerners rely on grains for a large part of their diet. Whether stopping for a snack at a roadside barbecue or feasting with friends, Nigerians know how to prepare colorful, diverse meals.

Some Nigerian Dishes

Jollof rice is a generally spicy dish with rice, tomatoes, onions, salt, red peppers, spices, and a mixture of vegetables and meat.

Suya is a meat kebab, and it's considered a national delicacy. The meat is coated with peanuts, chili pepper, and other spices and barbecued on a stick. You can find this treat all over Nigeria.

Groundnut Stew is peanut stew. It is made from a tomato and onion base served with beef, chicken, or fish and various vegetables.

Fried plantains often accompany main dishes are served as delicious snacks.

Mosa is a thick paste of fermented corn sprinkled with sugar.

Moi Moi is made from steamed black-eyed beans served as a pudding. Onions and black pepper are added, and the pudding is wrapped in a banana leaf.

Beverages include *kunu*, made with millet, sorghum, or maize; palm wine; and *zobo*, made from roselle juice, a variant of hibiscus.

Plantain

Holidays & Festivals

Nigerians celebrate several holidays throughout the year, including their Independence Day on October 1 and Workers Day on May 1. Depending on their religion, the people also celebrate traditional Islamic or Christian holidays.

New Year's Day • *January 1*

Mouloud (Birth of the Prophet) • *date varies*

Good Friday • *date varies*

Easter Monday • *date varies*

Worker's Day • *May 1*

Eid al-Fitr (End of Ramadan) • *date varies*

Independence Day • *October 1*

Eid al-Kabir (Feast of the Sacrifice) • *date varies*

Christmas Day • *December 25*

Boxing Day • *December 26*

Creative Arts

Literature

Nigeria is well-known for their post-colonial contributions to English literature. Wole Soyinka, the first African to receive the Nobel Laureate in Literature, and Chinua Achebe, author of the controversial novel *Things Fall Apart*, are two of Nigeria's most famous writers. Other internationally-known Nigerian writers include: Buchi Emecheta, Helon Habila, John Peppar Clark, Ken Saro Wiwa, Ben Okri, and Chimamanda Ngozi Adichie. After Egypt, Nigeria has the second largest newspaper market in Africa, circulating several million copies per day.

Music

Since Nigeria is home to so many ethnic groups and each group has its own musical techniques and instruments, the country produces a wide variety of music. Nigerian music combines native traditions with those brought by immigrants from the Congo, Brazil, and Cuba. Its native rhythms and popular music have become known worldwide. In the late 20th century, musicians like Fela Kuti combined Nigerian folk music with American jazz and soul to form music known as *Afrobeat*. King Sunny Adé made a type of music called *JuJu* famous by pairing percussion beats with traditional Yoruba music. Hip hop is becoming increasingly popular throughout the country. Nigeria received international recognition when MTV hosted Africa's first music award show in Abuja.

Film

In recent years the Nigerian film industry, nicknamed *Nollywood*, has generated much revenue from its productions. Its film studios are based in Lagos and Abuja and provide income for many.

In Your Classroom

Have students make instruments to create their own music by using cardboard toilet rolls, tape, and seeds to make noise-makers. Tupperware makes excellent drums. Be creative! Bring in a video camera and make a music video.

Listen to jazz music with your class and discuss the African influences in the music.

Sports & Games

Football is Nigeria's national sport and its team, the Super Eagles, have made World Cup appearances on several occasions. The country has a local Premier League and has won the African Cup of Nations as well as Olympic gold. Its Junior teams are extremely talented, having produced numerous celebrities over the years who have gone on to play in the European Champions League. Boxing, cricket, basketball, and track and field are also important sports in Nigeria.

In Your Classroom

Teach students a traditional Nigerian game known as *Nte-too*, which is similar to marbles. Instead of marbles, Nte-too uses seeds (use avocado or peach). Two players face each other, each kneeling behind a line of six to 12 seeds or nuts. Player One rolls his nut toward Player Two's line. If he hits a nut, he gets to keep it and continues his turn. If he does not hit a nut, Player Two gets to keep the nut and takes his turn rolling. In the end the player with the most nuts wins.

Rwanda

Welcome to Rwanda!

Rwanda is a small landlocked country in east central Africa. The country has been nicknamed "Land of a Thousand Hills" due to its rugged terrain. Conditions in Rwanda are cramped, as it is the most densely populated country on the continent.

FAST FACTS

Official Name: Republic of Rwanda

Location: Rwanda is situated in central Africa. It is bordered by Uganda to the north, Tanzania to the east, Burundi to the south, and the Democratic Republic of the Congo to the west.

Population: 11,370,425 (2010 estimate)

Capital city: Kigali

Area: 10,169 square miles

Major Languages: Kinyarwanda, French, and English are the official languages of Rwanda. But Kiswahili (Swahili) is used in commercial centers. Like many parts of Africa, universal Bantu words are also used to communicate.

Major Religions: Roman Catholic: 56.5%
Protestant: 26%
Adventist: 11.1%
Muslim: 44.6%

Currency: Rwandan *franc*

Climate: Rwanda experiences a temperate climate. The country has two rainy seasons, from February to April and from November to January.

The Land: The terrain is made up of mostly grassy hills and uplands.

Type of Government: Republic

Flag: The Rwandan flag is made up of three colors: green, yellow, and blue. A horizontal blue stripe covers the top half of the flag, with two smaller yellow and green stripes beneath it. A yellow sun sits in the blue upper right corner of the flag. The blue symbolizes peace and happiness, the yellow represents economic development, and the green represents hope for the future. The sun in the corner looks much like a sun in a blue sky and symbolizes enlightenment.

National Animal: African leopard

National Motto: *"Ubumwe, Umurimo, Gukunda Igihugu"* ("Unity, Work, Patriotism")

72

Natural Environment

Rwanda is bordered by Uganda in the north, Tanzania in the east, Burundi on the south, and Democratic Republic of the Congo on the west. Rwanda is mostly an agricultural and pastoral country. The elevation in this region averages over 5,000 feet and Rwanda's highest peak, Mount Karlsimbi, reaches 14,787 feet.

Significant bodies of water in Rwanda include: the Kagera River, Lake Tanganyika, and Lake Kivu. The central plateau is made up of the Savanna highlands, a deforested area with eroding grassland. The valleys and volcanoes in the northern part of the country contain the most fertile soil. Rwanda's Volcano National Park is known for its rare mountain gorillas, and Kagera National Park helps to preserve other native wildlife. Since Rwanda's national parks have proportionately more land than that of other African countries, the rising human population is facing challenges with the limited amount of land available to them.

On the land that is available, Rwandans grow crops such as coffee, tea, sweet potatoes, cassava, and bananas; or they raise livestock. The country's national resources include gold, tin, tungsten, beryl, methane, and hydropower. Although Rwanda periodically suffers from drought, the country is generally able to feed itself.

In Your Classroom

Have students locate Rwanda on a map of Africa. Using the map as a template, they should make their own Rwandan maps, labeling Kigali, Mount Karlsimbi, the Kagera River, and major lakes.

Using a large piece of poster board, let students work together to make a Rwandan flag to hang in the classroom.

A HISTORY OF RWANDA

Rwanda was first inhabited by the pastoral Tutsi and agricultural Hutu peoples. These groups, made up of many clans, began to form kingdoms in the 15th century. The Kingdom of Rwanda, ruled by a Tutsi dynasty, gained domination of the region through military expansion.

The region became a German protectorate in 1884. It was combined with another territory and became German East Africa. German personnel explored and settled in the region, influencing the ruling dynasty with advisors and missionaries. They favored Tutsi control of the region. In 1916, Belgian forces seized control of the area. After that it was known as the Ruanda-Urundi.

The Belgians tried to improve conditions in Rwanda through the institution of many projects, including agricultural, educational, and health initiatives. New crops were introduced to the country to manage a rising population. Like the Germans before them, the Belgians supported Tutsi dominance of Rwanda. This support would not last, however. During the 1940s, Tutsis who spoke out against Belgium and promoted independence were driven from the country.

After World War II, tensions increased between the dominant Tutsis and the Hutus. Belgium, steering the nation towards independence, switched sides and began supporting the Hutu population. The situation exploded in the Rwandan Revolution of 1959. The Hutus violently overthrew the Tutsi kingdom, forcing many Tutsis into exile in neighboring countries. In 1962, Rwanda gained its independence from Belgium. Grégoire Kayibanda, who had led the Hutu movement for power, was elected the nation's first president.

Peace in Rwanda was ever elusive. The Tutsis that had been exiled in 1959 staged attacks around the country, and the Hutus retaliated with violence against Tutsis still living in Rwanda. In 1973, Juvenal Habyarimana staged a successful military coup against the Kayabanda regime. Under his presidency, the country gained a small measure of stability.

But it wasn't to continue for long. The exiled Tutsis formed a rebel group called the Rwandan Patriotic Front (RPF) and invaded Rwanda, starting the Rwandan Civil War. Fighting continued until a ceasefire was signed in 1993, neither group having gained a significant edge. In 1994, President Habyarimana's plane was shot down, and the shaky truce was destroyed. Ethnic strife intensified and in 1994, the Rwandan Genocide was ordered by the government. Some 800,000 Tutsis and sympathetic Hutus were put to death. Fighting was renewed, and the RPF defeated the Hutus and stopped the killings.

The Hutus were afraid the Tutsis would punish them for what they had done, and so fled to neighboring countries. Most of the refugees returned to Rwanda, except for several thousand who stayed in the Congo, plotting to take back their country from the Tutsis.

International organizations and other countries have helped Rwanda attempt to recover from its violent history. The country established a legislative government which allows its people to vote, but ethnic tensions remain strong throughout the land. Rwanda's industries are not thriving and the people continue to struggle with racial turmoil.

Daily Life

Education

Originally, most of Rwanda's schools were established and run by Christian missionaries. Some of these private institutions still exist. Public education lasts for nine years. Six years are spent in primary school and three in a secondary program. The government hopes to extend provided education by 2015. Many Rwandan children, however, simply do not attend. Poverty and commitments at home often keep them away.

All Rwandans speak Kinyarwanda, but educated people speak French and English as well. In recent years, English has begun to replace French in its importance; it is now the language used to teach in schools.

Religion

Most Rwandans are Christians, with Protestant numbers increasing and Catholic numbers decreasing since the genocide of 1994. Evangelical Christian missionaries opposed genocide, helped the natives, and have continued to share their faith with them while helping the country rebuild and develop. Muslims comprise about 5% of the population, an increase since 1994 as well. This is largely due to the Muslim people helping save the lives of many Tutsis during Hutu attacks. A small percentage of Rwandans still maintain their traditional indigenous beliefs.

Language & Expressions

Famous Rwandan Proverbs

Here are some famous Rwandan proverbs. What do you think they mean?

He who has travelled alone can tell what he likes.

Every cackling hen was an egg first.

You can outdistance that which is running after you, but not what is running inside you.

In a court of fowls, the cockroach never wins his case.

Body Language and Etiquette in Rwanda

Here are some examples of body language and etiquette you will find in Rwanda.

You should always show respect when in the presence of elders.

When visiting someone in Rwanda, bring a small gift of chocolates, fruits, or toys for children.

Discussions often start with a great deal of small talk before getting serious. Don't be impatient to get to the main point. This will offend the person with whom you are speaking.

 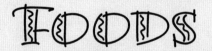

FOODS

Food is relatively simple in Rwanda. Staples include many of the crops grown in the region, like bananas, plantains, sweet potatoes, cassava, and beans. Potatoes are grown in a few areas, brought by German and Belgian colonists in the 19th century. Meat is not easy for many Rwandans to afford, and so it is eaten rarely. When it is consumed, it is usually beef, goat, or chicken. In certain regions, fish is popular.

National dishes are variations on these staple foods. *Ugali* is maize flour that is cooked until the texture is like porridge. This is rolled into a ball and dipped in vegetable or meat stews. *Matoke* are green bananas that are peeled and steamed, served with vegetable, peanut, or meat sauce. *Isombe* is mashed cassava leaves, often served with fish. Common beverages in Rwanda include milk, fruit juices, wine, and beer.

Holidays & Festivals

Rwandans celebrate a number of common public holidays, along with some specific to their country. At the end of each month, a national day of community service, known as *umuganda*, is observed.

New Year's Day • *January 1*

Heroes' Day • *February 1*

Good Friday • *date varies*

Genocide Memorial Day • *April 7*
(includes a week of mourning)

Labour Day • *May 1*

Independence Day • *July 1*

Liberation Day • *July 4*

Assumption • *August 15*

Feast of the Sacrifice • *date varies*

Christmas Day • *December 25*

Boxing Day • *December 26*

76

Creative Arts

Rwanda has a strong oral literary history. Storytelling has and continues to be a part of the country's culture. Very few books have been written in Rwanda's native language of Kinyarwanda, but many have been written in French. Alexis Kagame, a clergyman and historian, published a number of traditionally oral Rwandan poetry and mythology. Important books written after the genocide include: *Le Piège ethnique (The Ethnic Trap)* and *Le Feu sous la soutane (Fire under the Cassock)* by Benjamin Sehene. These books cover the events that led up to the genocide of 1994 and give accounts of several events that occurred during and after the genocide.

The music of Rwanda is similar to most African folk music. Traditional music and dance are taught in dance groups throughout the country. *Ballet National Urukerereza* is the most famous of these groups and performs at international functions. One of the most important and respected Rwandan music traditions is the *ikinimba*. This dance tells stories of Rwandan heroes and kings and is accompanied by traditional stringed musical instruments.

Before the genocide, Rwanda boasted many famous musicians and popular bands. Today, musician Jean-Paul Samputu and his group Ingeli perform neo-traditional Rwandan music with a Christian message. Their goal is to spread peace and raise support for Rwandan orphans. In 2003, they won two Kora awards (African Grammy) for "Best Traditional Artist" and "Most Inspiring Artist." Recently, Samputu and his group brought twelve Rwandan orphans on tour with them in America.

In Your Classroom

Assign the class a popular historical story. Divide the class into groups and have each group create an interpretive dance that tells the story and then perform it for the rest of the class.

As a class, discuss several current events that affect students today. Write these on the board. Have each student pick a topic and write a paragraph about it, making it as creative as possible. Encourage them to make it personal and write about how it has affected their life.

Tell Your Story

The history and culture of Rwanda are passed through generations by telling stories. Write your own story on the lines below. Where does your family come from? What traditions do you follow? How do you continue the history of your family?

◇◇◇

_____

_____

_____

_____

_____

_____

_____

_____

_____

_____

_____

_____

_____

_____

_____

_____

Somalia

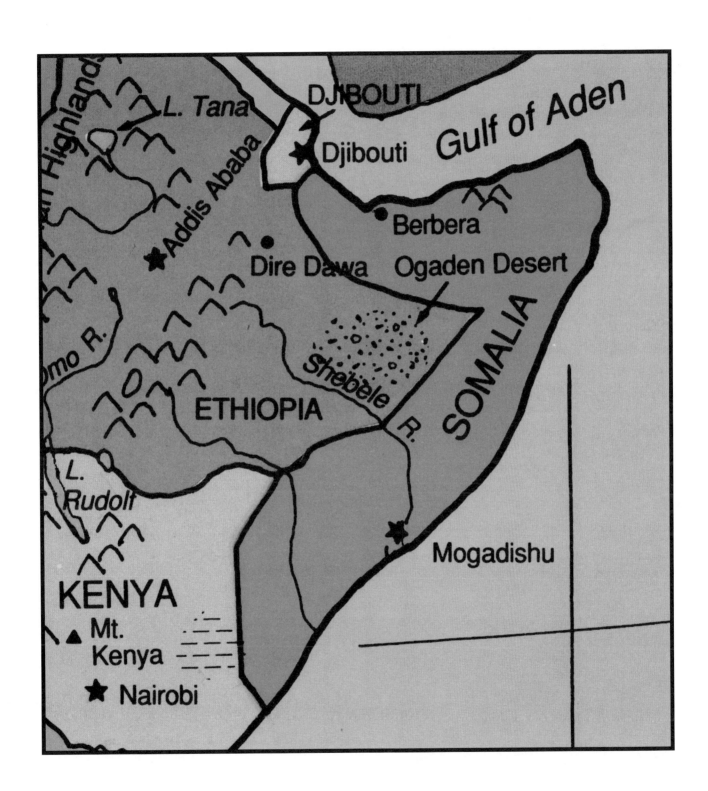

Welcome to Somalia!

Somalia is located on the Horn of Africa, the easternmost part of the continent. The country has a rich history. Once ruled by Italy and Britain, Somalia gained its independence in 1960. Most of the people are nomads, herding camels and living off the milk of their livestock.

FAST FACTS

Official Name: Somali Republic

Location: Somalia is located on the eastern tip of Africa, bordered by the Indian Ocean, the Gulf of Aden, Djibouti, Ethiopia, and Kenya.

Population: 9,925,640 (2010 estimate)

Capital City: Mogadishu

Area: 246,201 square miles

Major Language: Somali

Major Religion: Sunni Muslim

Currency: Somali *shilling*

Climate: Mostly, Somalia experiences a desert climate. Monsoons begin in December and end in May.

The Land: Most of the country is varied plateau, with hills in the north.

Type of Government: Parliamentary federal government (transitional)

Flag: The flag is a five-pointed white star on a bright blue field. The five-pointed star is symbolic of the five regions in the Horn of Africa (Ogaden, the Northern Frontier District, Djibouti, and the former Italian Somaliland and British Somaliland), and the light blue represents the Indian Ocean.

Coat of arms: The current Somali coat of arms features two leopards holding a shield painted in the colors of the flag.

National Animal: Leopard

80

Natural Environment

The northern portion of the country is desert, while the southern portion is coastal plains and plateaus. The desert extends to the Ogo and Migurtinia mountains. South of these mountains is the Ogo Plateau which turns into the Haud Plateau, an important grazing region. The arid southern coastal plains eventually lead to the more temperate Shebeli-Juba lowlands and plateau. Northern regions experience an average of three inches of rain per year, while the south receives 12-20 inches.

All of Somalia's significant rivers flow into the Indian Ocean, including the largest ones: the Juba and Webi Shabeelle, Daror and Nugaaleed. Fishing along the coast has become one of Somalia's few industries. The others are minor manufacturing centers and exporting livestock and livestock products. One of the most common herd animals is the camel. This is because they survive well in hot, desert-like conditions, as they are able to retain water in their humps for long periods of time, while other animals need water almost daily. Camels also produce milk, which is an important food source for Somali nomads.

In Your Classroom

Show students a map of the world or a globe. Have them locate Somalia. Using the globe, have them make their own map of the country, labeling major rivers, cities, and geographical points of interest, such as the desert and mountains.

Discuss the similarities between the Somali flag and other national flags. What do they have in common? Make a Somali flag to hang in the classroom next to a map of the country.

A History of Somalia

Arabs and Persians set up trading posts along the Gulf of Aden and the Indian Ocean during the seventh century. Somali nomads and pastoral Galla from southern Ethiopia began to arrive in present-day Somalia around the tenth century. Over the next 900 years, Somalis continued to spread across the Horn of Africa.

Between the 1880s and World War II, Britain and Italy controlled different parts of the country. Native Somalis fought against foreign influence and control with mixed results. Muhammad Abdullah Hassan, leader of the Dervish, led perhaps the fiercest resistance force against European invasion, particularly the British presence. Hassan rallied many Somalis to his cause, and fought from the end of the 19th century until his forces were defeated in 1920. Struggles continued between Somalis and Europeans, most notably the British and Italians.

After World War II, Britain gave part of Somalia to Ethiopia, although this region was heavily populated with Somalis. Over the next decade, Italy and Britain gradually handed control of Somalia over to their respective protectorates and territories. In 1960, both the British and Italian sectors were granted independence, and the two joined together on July 1, 1960, to form the Somali Republic.

A civilian government ruled the country for the next nine years. Then a military coup placed President Muhammad Siad Barré into power. In 1976, he created the Somali Revolutionary Socialist party. Over the next decade, Somalia and Ethiopia fought over their land. Sometimes Ethiopia controlled a territory and sometimes Somalia did. In 1988, the two countries signed a nonaggression agreement. President Siad Barré was reelected in 1986 but was accused of human rights violations. Riots in Mogadishu in 1989 reflected national tension. Thousands of Somalis escaped to Ethiopia for refuge.

After Siad Barré's regime ended in 1991, the country became a place of tumult. Violence, riots, and anarchy broke out across Somalia. Different regions formed their own separate states, declaring their independence from the rest of the country. With the help of other governments and international organizations such as the UN, Somalia has strived to achieve a peaceful existence among its people. They have not yet been successful, but the hope is that a stable government will be established and the Somali people will be able to live in harmony with one another and those on their borders.

Daily Life

The Nomadic Life

Most Somalis are nomads who travel through the country with herds of livestock. Camels are common herding animals in Somalia. Families travel together and everyone does their part. Parents tend to have many children (an average of six per family). These children grow up with heavy responsibilities. At a very young age a Somali child may take the family herd through the savanna and desert in search of water sources.

Since nomads are always traveling and rarely stay in the same place for very long, their homes are portable. Much like the Native American's tepees, Somali homes are temporary and can be easily assembled or taken down when the family is ready to move somewhere new. The mother's job is to take care of the home, make meals for her family, and care for the younger children not yet old enough to help with the herds. The mother retains her last name and affiliation with her clan. The father's job is to hunt for food.

Somali children take on their father's last name and clan affiliation. Boys are very valuable to the family because they will help their fathers provide. Girls are valuable helpers as well and hope to make advantageous marriages to help their families. Marriages are usually arranged and the bride is often significantly younger than her husband. People tend to arrange marriages within their own clan to strengthen loyalty and family ties. As is the custom among many native Africans, a bride is bought with a *dowry*—a payment to her father, typically in livestock.

Somali families who are more fortunate help their relatives who are in need. Families who live in cities might take in relatives' children. Nomadic families who have more food and livestock typically share with those who do not have enough.

Because war has disrupted the country for so long, organized sports are virtually nonexistent. Young Somalis enjoy playing soccer, but there is no league or team for them to join.

Education

Since the government collapsed in 1991, the education system has transitioned from public to private. Puntland and Somaliland regions both offer free primary schooling. In the last several years, primary school enrollment has increased because of this.

82

Somalis living in cities have easier access to an education. Nomads are often unable to attend school. The only education systems they are able to attend are the Qur'anic schools, which offer basic religious instruction.

Somalia offers several universities, primarily in the large cities. Three of their universities are ranked in the top 100 institutions in Africa.

Religion

The Islamic faith is divided into two main sects: the Sunni and the Shia. These sects differ on several issues, the main one being their interpretation of the holy book of Islam, the Qur'an (or Koran.) The Qur'an was written by Mohammad, who was inspired by Allah to instruct others in Islamic teachings.

Mosque

Nearly all Somalis are Sunni Muslims. Muslims believe in the five pillars of Islam: there is one God, Allah, and Mohammad is his prophet; giving to the poor; daytime fasting during the month of Ramadan; making at least one pilgrimage to Mecca; and praying five times a day. Muslim places of worship are called mosques. Mosques ring their bells five times a day to call Muslims to pray.

Islam entered Somalia early on, possibly even before it became fully established in Mecca. The prophet Mohammad urged a group of persecuted Muslims to cross the Red Sea into Africa to find religious freedom. These Sunni Muslims settled in the Horn of Africa, present day Somalia.

In Your Classroom

Make a model of a nomad home. Use Popsicle sticks, glue, cloth, and toy animals to create the dwelling and the herd.

Many African women carry food and supplies from one place to another in baskets balanced on their head. Have the students practice balancing baskets or other items, such as books, on their heads. Ask them to imagine and discuss using this as a means of carrying things.

Discuss some of the most common religions in the world (Christianity, Islam, Hindu, Buddhism, Judaism, etc.) What do the students know about these religions? Compare what these religions have in common by making a chart with different categories such as "place of worship" and "book of faith." Discuss their differences. On a map, label parts of the world where each religion is most prominent.

Language & Expressions

Famous Somali Proverbs

Here are some famous Somali proverbs. What do you think they mean?

One refusing a sibling's advice breaks his arm.

A brave man dies once, a coward a thousand times.

A dog which refuses a bone is not alive.

A madman does not lack wisdom.

A man throws stones, not words.

Either be a mountain or lean on one.

Somalis don't say a false proverb.

Body Language and Etiquette in Somalia

Here are some examples of body language and etiquette you will find in Somalia.

When in Somalia, you might be invited to milk a cow. Seriously! This is a polite way of being greeted by Somalis. They are offering you a drink from their own livestock. It's a great honor.

Among certain Somalis, Arab hand gestures are used to communicate.

Do not use your left hand when eating in Somalia. This is very rude and inappropriate.

Somali

Most of the country's population is Somali and most of them are nomads who herd their livestock through Somalia, Kenya, and Ethiopia. The Somalis are divided into two groups: the Sab in the south and the Somal in the north. Since nearly all of the country's population is Somali, almost everyone speaks the official language of Somali. The language was introduced in written form in 1972. Arabic, English, and Italian are also spoken in Somalia.

Here are a few Somali words and phrases:

English	Somali	Pronunciation
Good morning	Subax Wanaagsan	"Subah Wanaksin"
Good night	Habeen Wanaagan	"Habayn Wanaksin"
Hello	Iska Waran	"Iska Warran"
Goodbye	Jaaw	"Chow"
Do you speak English?	Ma Ku Hadli Kartaa Ingiriisi?	"Mak Hadlee Karta Ingreezee?"
What is your name?	Magacaa?	"Maga-a?"
Yes	Haa	"Ha"
No	May	"My"

In Your Classroom

Have students practice saying the Somali words and pronunciations. Try to engage in a simple conversation.

Somalis Muslims do not drink alcohol, eat pork, or consume anything that died on its own. Typically, they eat dinner after 9 PM. During the month of Ramadan, Muslims do not eat during the daytime, so their dinner is often much later—sometimes not until 11 PM.

At mealtimes, families gather together and sit around a large plate or mat. Men are served first and the women and children eat later. Small children eat out of their mother's hand. When eating, Somalis only use their right hand. The left hand is used for matters of personal hygiene and it is therefore considered rude to use it when eating.

Breakfast

Somalis usually eat pancake-style bread called *canjeero* for breakfast. The bread is served with *ghee*, a kind of butter, and sugar. It is sometimes accompanied by a side dish of liver, goat meat, beef, or a mixture of goat and camel meat called jerky. Tea, called *shah*, is usually drunk.

An alternative morning meal is *polenta*, a porridge served with butter or sugar.

Lunch

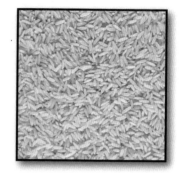

Rice is the main ingredient of lunches in Somalia. It's frequently spiced with cumin, sage, cloves, or other flavor enhancer, and is served in stews or with a side of meat or banana. Steak and fish are eaten in some parts of the country, as are cornmeal and pasta.

One unique dish, known as *Federation*, is a mixture of spaghetti and rice layered with meat, vegetables, salad, and a banana.

Dinner

Cambuulo, a dish made with cooked azuki beans, butter, and sugar, is a one of Somalia's most popular dinnertime meals. Specially seasoned rice and pasta are also enjoyed throughout the country. Dinners are often complemented with *muufo*, or cornbread.

In Your Classroom

Have your students eat their lunch with one hand. Discuss different customs of eating, such as manners and etiquette, that students experience at home and elsewhere.

Holidays & Festivals

Most of the holidays celebrated in Somalia are Islamic in origin. The country also celebrates several public national holidays.

Public Holidays (based on the Gregorian calendar)

New Year • *January 1*

Labour Day • *May 1*

Independence from the United Kingdom • *July 1*

Independence Day • *July 4*

Religious Holidays (based on the Islamic lunar calendar)

The dates of these holidays vary.

Birthday of Muhammad

Muhammad's Ascension to Heaven

End of Ramadan

Muslim New Year

Ashura

Writing

Somali scholars have produced vast amounts of Islamic poetry and *Hadith* – oral traditions from Mohammad's life. Their writings make up the majority of Somali literature. When Somalia became a written language in 1972, numerous authors wrote books that became huge successes. One of the most successful authors, Nuruddin Farah, wrote the novels *From a Crooked Rib* and *Links*, which helped him achieve the Neustadt International Prize for Literature in 1998.

Music

Traditional Somali music combined with modern rock, hip hop, jazz, and other beats has grown in popularity. One well-known Somali musician, K'naan, resides in Toronto, Canada. He sings about the country's struggles during the civil war. Because of political instability, the center of the Somali music industry moved from the country's capital, Mogadishu, to Toronto. Many Somalis live there, as well as Columbus, Ohio; Minneapolis, Minnesota; and London, England.

Art

Carving
The art of carving is called *qoris* in Somalia. Wood and marble carvers were active in the region in the medieval period, and carvings can be seen on the surfaces of ancient mosques. The nomadic people of Somalia have been practicing wood carving for centuries. Especially popular is the elaborate carving of exterior and interior parts of architecture, especially doors, shutters, and sills.

Architecture
The various stone structures from Somalia's past are works of art in their own right. Cities, castles and fortresses, mosques and temples, lighthouses, and even tombs exist throughout the country. Of particular interest is the study of mosques, in which can be seen many different progressions of style and form.

South Africa

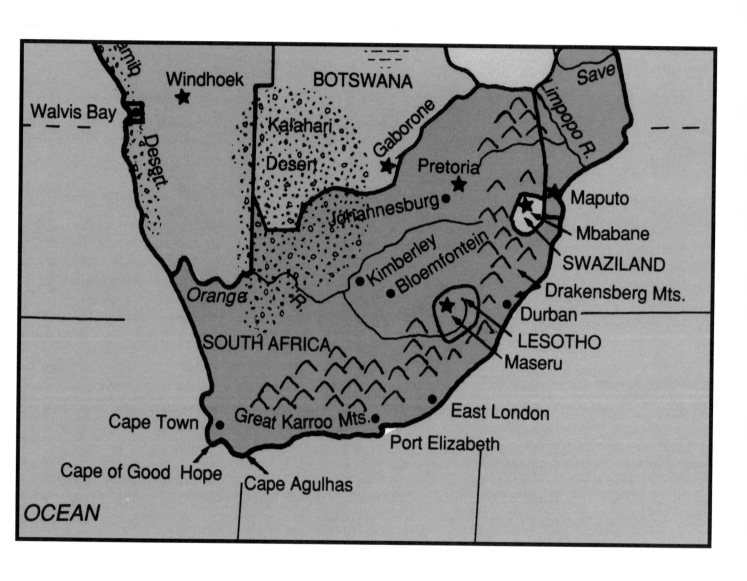

OCEAN

South Africa – MP5122

Welcome to South Africa!

FAST FACTS

Official Name: The Republic of South Africa

Location: South Africa is found at the southern tip of the African continent.

Population: 49,004,031 (2010 estimate)

Capital Cities: South Africa has three capital cities: Pretoria is the executive capital, Bloemfontein the judicial capital, and Cape Town the legislative capital.

Area: 471,445 square miles

Major Language: South Africa has 11 official languages: Afrikaans, English, Ndebele, Northern Sotho, Sotho, Swazi, Tswana, Tsonga, Venda, Xhosa, and Zulu. Afrikaans, Xhosa, and Zulu are the most widely spoken, even though English is the language of commerce.

Major Religions: A variety of Christian denominations make up about 80 percent of Muslim faiths. No religious affiliation: 15%

Currency: the South African *rand*

Climate: A mostly semiarid climate, with a subtropical east coast, allows for warm days and cool nights.

The Land: A large interior plateau is surrounded by hills.

Type of Government: Republic

Flag: South Africa has a very colorful flag with a unique pattern. Many people dispute the symbolism behind the colors, as there is no official description. However, the different colors are generally believed to represent the diverse elements of the South African people. The Y pattern brings to mind converging roads that move forward as one. It could be said that the flag symbolizes all of the diverse elements of the country's population coming together as one and marching into the future.

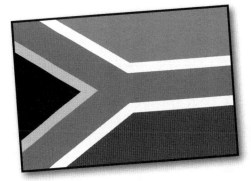

South Africa's law says the flag should always be treated with "dignity and respect." When handling the flag, there are certain rules people must abide by. Some of these include: never letting the flag touch the ground, never using it as a table cloth, never using it to cover a statue or plaque, never draping it in front of a platform, never using it at unveiling ceremonies, or using it to start or finish a competition of any kind. The President of South Africa must give approval for any manufactured or reproduced flag. The flag should be raised at sunrise and lowered at sunset, and is only allowed to fly at night if it is lit up. When people are present while a flag is being raised or lowered, they must remove their hats and place their right hand over their hearts. The flag is only flown upside down as a distress signal.

National Animal: Springbok

National Motto: "Diverse people unite"

Natural Environment

South Africa is home to diverse landscapes and resources. The Cedarberg, Swartberg, and Baviannskloof are a group of sedimentary mountain ranges that combine together to form the Cape Ranges. In the east, the Drakensberg Mountains contain the country's highest peak, Injasuti (11,181 feet). The entire range of mountains are known for their spectacular height; in winter, heavy snowfall often blocks the mountain passes, making the area treacherous. The Drakensberg separate the coastal lowlands of the Cape and Natal from the Highveld (the name for the elevated interior plateaus).

The Highveld's elevations range between 4,000 to 6,000 feet and are home to the gold-bearing Witwatersrand mountains. The Highveld not only contains much of the country's gold supply, but most of its other mineral wealth as well, including diamonds, coal, iron ore, copper, and manganese.

Along the northwest border, South Africa shares part of the Kalahari Desert with neighboring Botswana. The Great Karoo, a semiarid basin of buttes and mesas, lies between the Cape Ranges and the Drakensberg mountains.

Due to inadequate rainfall and broken terrain, none of South Africa's rivers are navigable. The Limpopo River in the north forms part of the country's northern border with Botswana, Zimbabwe and Mozambique. The Orange River and its two main tributaries, the Vaal and the Caledon, drain the interior plateau. Occasionally, people divert the Orange River around the cities of Bloemfontein and Kimberley to the Cape coast. This is usually for agricultural, urban or industrial uses and is part of the Orange River Project. The project consisted of constructing dams and canals in order to provide irrigation and hydroelectric power to parts of the country.

Because the soil is not very fertile and much of it, especially in the Drakensberg, has severely eroded, the country does not have many natural forests. Reforestation projects are underway to attempt to combat this problem. Despite the lack of trees, South Africa boasts rich and diverse wildlife. Elephants, giraffes, zebras, rhinoceroses, antelope, and other wildlife make South Africa their home and are protected in game reserves throughout the country. The country also has many types of birds and over 100 species of snakes!

A safari in South Africa

In Your Classroom

The South African flag is colorful and complicated. Have students make one to hang in the classroom using construction paper, scissors, glue, and poster board. Place it in a prominent place or beside a map of South Africa.

Make a map of South Africa and hang it in your classroom. Be sure to label and color the different regions of the country. Include major cities and rivers.

Discuss the various rules associated with South Africa's flag. Quiz the students on their knowledge of the rules for their flag. Explain why it is important to show respect for such an important national symbol. Make two lists to help you compare the rules for your flag and the South African flag.

A History of South Africa

The first known inhabitants of South Africa were San and Khoiki hunters. Between 1000 and 1500 CE, the Bantu-speaking people began journeying south and establishing themselves in present-day South Africa. In 1488, Bartolomeu Dias led a group of Portuguese mariners around the Cape of Good Hope on their way to the Far East. In 1652, Dutch spice traders landed at the tip of southern Africa, establishing Cape Town as a stopping point between the Netherlands and Asia. Britain eventually took over the Cape of Good Hope in 1806, forcing the Dutch settlers (known as Boers) northward to settle new regions.

Later that century, gold and diamonds were discovered in South Africa, increasing fortune-seeking immigration and subjugation of the natives. From 1899-1902, the British and Boers (later called the Afrikaners) fought each other over the land, with the British emerging victorious; however, after the South Africa Act of 1909, the two groups ruled together under the Union of South Africa.

In the 1948 elections, the National Party came into power. They furthered a system set up by previous officials called *apartheid*. Apartheid meant separate development of the races and was designed to ensure white supremacy. Over the next several decades, this racist policy treated blacks unfairly, assigning their race to certain parts of the country and making sure all cities were racially segregated, giving the white population the more desirable places to live. Blacks had to carry passbooks whenever they went into "white" regions of the country for more than 72 hours. Apartheid left the "black" regions of the country underdeveloped and economically disadvantaged with high unemployment. Apartheid even went so far as to take away many blacks' citizenships. Opposition to apartheid caused violent riots and revolts in which many South Africans lost their lives.

In 1961, South Africa ceased to be a commonwealth. It became a republic. The government elected to continue the legal practice of apartheid. They did so despite growing worldwide disapproval. Several countries refused to deal with South Africa. Within the country, unrest was on the rise, and protest became louder and more frequent. Interactions between both sides became more violent, until open fighting and bombing began. An organization known as the African National Congress (ANC) was one major force of protest.

In January, 1974, the Mahlabatini Declaration of Faith was signed, laying the groundwork for a peaceful multiracial society governed for the good of all. By 1990, legitimate steps were taken, beginning the sharing of political power and ending racial discrimination and segregation. Groups like the ANC were legally recognized, and discrimination was dismantled. These negotiations took place between State President F.W. de Klerk and Nelson Mandela. Mandela, a member of the ANC and an anti-apartheid activist, had spent 27 years in prison for sabotage. Apartheid finally ended in 1994, with the first multi-racial elections bringing black majority to rule. Mandela became the republic's first democratic president. He was later awarded the Nobel Peace Prize.

Nelson Mandela

Tension is still present among the ANC and the rest of the country. In recent years, fighting came to a crisis, with ANC President Thabo Mbeki resigning in 2008. Aside from racial tension, South Africa also suffers from the HIV/AIDS epidemic. It has the highest number of deaths due to this virus, more than any other country in the world. South Africa has come a very long way from the horrors of apartheid, but it still has progress to make.

Nelson Mandela

Nelson Mandela is perhaps the greatest figure in South African history. Research the life and accomplishments of this man. Write a short biography of Mandela below.

◇◇

_____

_____

_____

_____

_____

_____

_____

_____

_____

_____

_____

_____

_____

_____

_____

Education

South Africa places a high importance on education, with its government spending 20 percent of its expenditures on education each year. South Africa offers 13 years of education. The first ten years of school are mandatory, but the last three are optional. In order for a student to go on to study at the university, he or she must pass the "matric exams" during the last year of high school. Once students have finished this final year and passed their exams, they are said to have "matriculated" (graduated) or received their "Matriculation Endorsement." Students who graduate from high school without passing their matric exams receive a Senior Certificate without matriculation endorsement.

South African universities are not run by the government, but rather their own councils. Some only require a Matriculation Endorsement to enter and others set additional requirements for incoming students. Unfortunately, effects from apartheid are still present; black South Africans sometimes do not receive as much higher education as whites or Indians.

Although English is used for much of the country's communication, it is just one of 11 official languages of South Africa, and is only the fifth most widely spoken. Other languages include: Pedi, Sotho, Tswana, Swazi, Venda, Tsonga, Afrikaans, Ndebele, Xhosa and Zulu. The most widely spoken language is Zulu (almost 24% of the population speaks this), followed by Xhosa and Afrikaans. Only 8% of South Africans speak English. Along with these 11 official languages, South Africa has many more unofficial languages as well as several European languages that are widely spoken.

Famous South African Proverbs

Here are some famous South African proverbs. What do you think they mean?

Not everyone who chased the zebra caught it, but he who caught it chased it.

It is the chef who knows the contents of the pot the best.

A fool is a wise man's ladder.

As great birds die the eggs rot.

Old age does not announce itself.

Body Language and Etiquette in South Africa

When greeting a South African, shake hands, smile, and maintain eye contact.

For 21st and 40th birthdays, it is traditional for South Africans to be given lavish gifts.

Always bring a gift, like wine or flowers, to a host's home.

In general, dress in South Africa is less casual.

The long list of countries and cultures that have been involved in South Africa's development and history has added much to the region, and cuisine is no exception. The fare in South Africa is often referred to as Rainbow Cuisine because of the variety of styles present.

Traditional South African cuisine is a big part of the mix. Meat is arguably the most important element in any meal. Beef, chicken, mutton, goat, and other meat are the center of most meals. On weekends, it's common to attend a barbecue (*braai*). The various meats dishes might be accompanied by *pap*, a traditional maize porridge served with meat gravy. Vegetables might also be served, like beans, pumpkin, or cabbage, but only as a side item – meat is king. If you ever have a South African to dinner, don't dare serve him or her a vegetarian meal! Such a gesture might be considered rude.

The importance of meat to South Africans is apparent at special occasions and events like weddings. It is likely that an animal will be purchased, slaughtered, and prepared just for the occasion.

Curry

The remaining stripes in South Africa's Rainbow Cuisine have been filled in by the many settlers, colonists, and immigrants that have made the country their home over the centuries. These foreign visitors brought different crops, tastes, and inspiration to the existing diet of South Africa. Cape Dutch is an excellent example of a cooking style brought to the country from elsewhere. The Dutch brought not only their culinary contributions, but also those of their many slaves. Cape Dutch cuisine is characterized by its use of spice. Highlights include curries, pickled fish, fish stews, and *sambal*, a chili-based sauce used as a condiment (like ketchup or mustard, only spicier).

South Africans enjoy dining out at the many restaurants in the country. Many of these eateries serve foreign food, further diversifying the diet of the country. Western fast food has also made its way into the region.

Holidays & Festivals

Here are some holidays celebrated throughout South Africa.

New Year's Day • *January 1*

Human Rights Day • *March 21*

Good Friday • *date varies*

Family Day • *date varies*

Freedom Day • *April 27* • celebrates the post-apartheid elections of 1994

Workers' Day • *May 1*

Youth Day • *June 16* • commemorates the Soweto riots of 1976 (in which South African youths were killed)

National Women's Day • *August 9* • celebrates a women's march against apartheid injustices in 1956

Heritage Day • *September 24* • all South Africans celebrate the many cultures that make up this diverse nation

Day of Reconciliation • *December 16* • instituted after the end of apartheid, a day to celebrate the rebuilding of the South African nation as a unified people under one flag

Christmas Day • *December 25*

Day of Goodwill (Boxing Day) • *December 26*

In Your Classroom

Have students select one of the distinctly South African holidays above. They should research the history behind the holiday, as well as ways that the day is celebrated. Have students present their findings to the class in a short oral presentation.

Music

The South African music scene is comprised of two main forms: pop and folk. In the 1920s, a type of music called *Marabi* developed in the slums of Johannesburg. Marabi was played on the piano and accompanied by a can filled with pebbles. Over the next decade, the style expanded and began using banjos and guitars. African jazz and jive sprung from this Marabi style of music.

Gospel and a cappella are also popular styles, as well as *Afrikaans*, which is a mixture of Dutch folk music with German and French influences. At first, Afrikaans music was melodramatic and sorrowful, but today it has evolved into a more lively style that is one of the best-sellers in the South African music scene.

In the mid-1980s a new music genre known has *Kwaito* appeared, rapidly becoming one of the most popular genres in the country. Kwaito is not just music, but a political force taking over radio, television, magazines, and influencing disc jockeys and the general population with its social economical form.

Literature

South Africa's first Nobel Peace Prize winner was Albert Luthuli in 1960, author of the book *Let My People Go*. The country also boasts several other prominent and internationally known black, white, and Afrikaner writers. During apartheid, all published work was strictly censored. The government controlled the media and used television and radio to communicate its own views and further its own agenda. Foreign journalists were not allowed to write freely about their experiences in South Africa, but had to submit their work to the South African government to review before it could be published abroad.

In Your Classroom

Form a Marabi band. If you are able, borrow a keyboard from the music room. Fill a plastic bottle with gravel and use it to accompany the piano. Create your own Marabi music together as a class.

Have the students pretend they are journalists during apartheid. Have them describe what they are experiencing and the difficulties that surround them. When they have finished, collect the stories and edit them as though you are the South African government. Return the stories back to the students and have them see what their censored writing looks like. Is it similar at all to what they intended? Discuss with them what it would be like to be a reporter or journalist during this time.

Soccer, cricket and rugby are the most popular sports in South Africa. Other sports, such as swimming, golf, track and field, tennis, netball, surfing, skateboarding, and basketball are also popular. South Africa is home to many famous sports starts including golfer Gary Player, who won the Career Grand Slam, boxers Brian Mitchell and "Baby Jake" Jacob Matlala, rugby stars like Francois Pienaar, Formula 1 motor racing world champion Jody Scheckter, the 2004 Olympic gold medal-winning 4x100 meter freestyle relay swimming team, and several footballers, including Quinton Fortune, Benni McCarthy and many others.

The country has hosted some important sporting championships in recent years. In 1995, South Africa hosted and won the Rugby World Cup championship, winning again in 2007. It also hosted the 2003 Cricket World Cup and the 2010 FIFA World Cup. The 2010 World Cup was the first championship ever held on the continent of Africa.

Zimbabwe

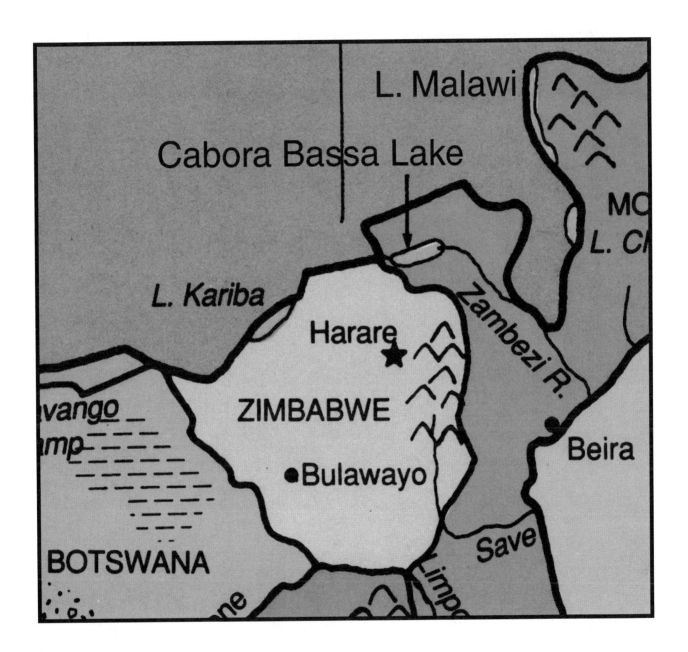

Welcome to Zimbabwe!

Zimbabwe is a landlocked country in southern Africa. It experiences a tropical climate, with cooler temperatures in the elevated regions. Because of its infertile soil and irregular rainfall, most of the country cannot be farmed. Zimbabwe is home to many ancient ruins and interesting natural formations, such as Balancing Rocks and Victoria Falls.

FAST FACTS

Official name: Republic of Zimbabwe

Location: Zimbabwe is in southern Africa. It is bordered by South Africa to the south, Botswana to the southwest, Zambia to the northwest, and Mozambique to the east.

Population: 12,084,304 (2010 estimate)

Capital City: Harare

Area: 150,871 square miles

Major Languages: English is the official language, but *Shona* (a Bantu language) and *Ndebele* are also widely spoken.

Major Religion: 50 percent of Zimbabweans practice *syncretic* religion, or a combination of Christian and indigenous beliefs. 25 percent are identified as strictly Christian, and 24 percent are Muslim.

Currency: Zimbabwean *dollar*

Climate: Zimbabwe experiences a tropical climate, with a rainy season taking place between November and March.

The Land: Much of the country is made up of high plateaus, which rise in the central regions. There are mountains in the east.

Type of Government: Parliamentary democracy

Flag: The Zimbabwean flag is green, yellow, black, red, and white. A soapstone bird on the left side of the flag represents a small statue of a bird found at the ruins of Great Zimbabwe, symbolizing the country's history. The red star underneath the bird represents the nation's struggle for peace and freedom.

Coat of Arms: The coat of arms features two *kudus* (antelope) standing upon wheat, cotton, and maize. Between the animals, a green shield depicts 14 waves of white and blue, symbolizing Victoria Falls. There is also a depiction of the Kingdom of Great Zimbabwe. A hoe and rifle are crossed behind the shield, and the flag's Great Zimbabwe Bird sits on a red star above it all.

National Animal:	Sable antelope
National Flower:	Flame lily
National Motto:	"Unity, Freedom, Work"

Natural Environment

Most of Zimbabwe's terrain is a high plateau called the Highveld. It is interrupted by a 300-mile mineral-enriched mountainous region known as the Great Dyke. The lowland regions in the Zambezi River valley and Sabi-Lundi and Limpopo river basins are called the Lowveld. These regions along with some areas with higher elevations in the east are the least populated parts of Zimbabwe.

Because of its elevation, temperatures in the Highveld are moderate. The Lowveld is much warmer. The Inyanga and Chimanimani mountains in the east are home to Zimbabwe's highest peak, Mount Inyangani, at 8,507 feet. This region experiences plenty of rainfall, while the semiarid southeastern region receives less than 20 inches of precipitation annually. Rainfall in Zimbabwe is usually too variable for growing crops, except in the eastern highlands and the Highveld areas.

The Zambezi River, the main river in Zimbabwe, is dammed at Kariba to form Lake Kariba, a body of water that provides hydroelectric power to Zimbabwe and Zambia. The Highveld is covered by savanna grasslands where baobab and teak trees grow. The Highveld is also home to the richer soils whereas the rest of the country generally has infertile sandy soils. Because most of Zimbabwe's land is not arable, the country must rely on mineral exports, mining, and tourism as its main money-earning industries.

Zimbabwe used to have the largest number of black rhinoceros in the world, but now the animals are disappearing. This is mostly due to poachers—people who trespass on private property and illegally kill the animals protected there.

Victoria Falls, some of the largest waterfalls in the world, are located between the Zimbabwe and Zambia border. The Falls are one of the Seven Natural Wonders of the World. David Livingstone, a Scottish explorer and Christian missionary, is believed to be the first European to see them.

Zimbabwe is also famous for its massive ruins from the Iron Age. These ruins, located south of modern-day Masvingo, were a religious and trading center from 950-1450 CE. Spiritually significant artifacts including female fertility figurines and soapstone bird carvings were found at this site.

The Rhodesian Ridgeback

The Rhodesian Ridgeback, also called the African Lion Hound, originated in Zimbabwe. These dogs are large and golden brown, with a distinct ridge of hair on their spine. This ridge is formed by hair that grows in the reverse direction of the rest of its coat. Native Zimbabwe tribes used these dogs for hunting (particularly lions), retrieving, guarding their property and taking care of their children. Rhodesian Ridgebacks are beautiful, intelligent dogs that are now popular pets around the world. While they are ferocious hunters in the wild, they are gentle, obedient dogs at home.

In Your Classroom

Bring a map or globe to school and have students find Zimbabwe. Then have each student make their own map of the country, drawing the significant rivers and cities. Staple this map to a folder where they can put worksheets or other information about Zimbabwe as they study it.

Have each student make their own Zimbabwe flag and color it. Staple this to the other side of their Zimbabwe folder.

Show the class pictures of Victoria Falls. Compare them to pictures of Niagara Falls. Have the students research the two waterfalls and discover which one is taller and which is wider.

Victoria Falls

Niagara Falls

Name _____   Date _____

Make a Zimbabwe Brochure

Zimbabwe is full of beautiful nature and wildlife. Design a photo brochure for Zimbabwe below. Find pictures of the country's plants, animals, and sights in magazines or on the Internet. Cut them out and paste them in the space below.

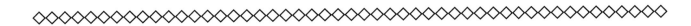

Visit Beautiful Zimbabwe!

A History of Zimbabwe

Archeological evidence shows that the Bantu people arrived in the modern-day region of Zimbabwe after the fifth century CE. In 1890, gold-seekers from the British South Africa Company crossed over the border in search of land and riches. These pioneers controlled the region, known as Rhodesia, until it became Southern Rhodesia—a self-governing British Colony. Despite its self-government, Britain had a right to intervene on constitutional and social issues.

In 1953, Southern Rhodesia, Northern Rhodesia, and Nyasaland joined together to form the Federation of Rhodesia and Nyasaland with Salisbury (now Harare) as the capital. This new nation adopted a constitution in 1961 which gave most of the power to whites and limited the voting rights of blacks. In 1963, blacks established their own governments in Northern Rhodesia (modern day Zambia) and Nyasaland (now Malawi). In 1965, the Rhodesian government declared its independence, but neither the United Kingdom nor any other country, except South Africa, recognized this breakaway colony. Guerilla warfare and trade sanctions imposed by the United Nations eventually led to free elections in 1979 and an independent Zimbabwe in 1980.

Robert Mugabe became the country's first prime minister and in 1987, became its first and only president. In 2000, Mugabe began a haphazard land redistribution campaign which caused many unhappy white farmers to leave. As a result, the nation's economy suffered greatly and many people could not even get basic commodities. In 2002, Mugabe rigged the presidential elections so he would win again, although the international community strongly condemned his actions. The ZANU-PF party won the parliamentary elections in 2005 by illegal means. This party abused their position to amend the constitution whenever they felt like it.

Mugabe and the government are responsible for human rights violations and many more corrupt actions that have outraged the Zimbabwean nation and the rest of the world. In 2008, it appeared as though a new president, Morgan Tsvangirai, was going to be elected and things would change; however, violence against Tsvangirai's party (the Movement for Democratic Change), ballot tampering, and other suspicious voting results caused the rest of the world to condemn the electoral process. After many difficult negotiations, a power-sharing agreement was reached that stated Mugabe would remain as president and Tsvangirai would become the prime minister. Because of political violence and corruption over the past few decades, many Zimbabweans have sought refuge in neighboring countries or migrated abroad.

Daily Life

Zimbabwean families typically have between three and four children. Most children attend school, but because of rising tuition and uniform expenses, some are unable to afford it. Family gatherings such as weddings, births, or graduations are important and should be properly celebrated. Zimbabweans usually do this by killing a goat or cow and having a large family barbecue or roast. Socializing with one's extended family is an important part of Zimbabwean life.

Education

Zimbabwe has one of the highest literacy rates in Africa. About 90% of adults can read and write, but that number is slowly decreasing. Most children attend schools run by the government that cost money to attend. Wealthier families often choose to send their children to independent schools, as these are not run by the government. Students are required to attend seven years of primary school and six years of secondary school before they are eligible for university. Zimbabweans attend school 40 weeks per year, from January to December. The school year is broken into three terms with each term divided by a one-month holiday.

After passing national examinations, students may choose to enter university and study in their country or abroad. Zimbabwe is home to several universities, with the University of Zimbabwe as the oldest and largest. Zimbabwe has produced many excellent scholars, politicians, doctors and accountants. Unfortunately, recent famine and financial issues have threatened the education system in Zimbabwe.

Religion

Fifty percent of Zimbabweans believe in a mixture of Christian and indigenous faiths. Twenty-five percent are Christian, 24% practice indigenous religions, and 1% believe in Islam or other religions. Ancestor worship is a common indigenous practice. The *Mbira Dza Vadzimu* (or "Voice of the Ancestors") is an instrument used at religious ceremonies throughout Africa.

Language & Expressions

Famous Zimbabwean Proverbs

Here are some famous Zimbabwean proverbs. What do you think they mean?

A borrowed fiddle does not finish the tune.

A grilled locust is better than no soup.

Don't throw out the old pot until you have the tinker make a new one.

If you can walk you can dance, if you can talk you can sing.

The old man gives the best advice.

Body Language and Etiquette in Zimbabwe

Here are some examples of body language and etiquette you will find in Zimbabwe.

In Zimbabwe, the older person always begins a greeting. Do not speak first when meeting an elder. Conversely, feel free to speak first when greeting a younger person.

Zimbabweans commonly use a three-part handshake specific to Africa. A standard handshake is followed by a grasping of thumbs and another standard handshake.

When speaking to someone over 50 years of age, call him an old man – seriously! The term madulla (old man) is a title of respect. You should call older women grannies (gogo).

Although English is the official language, mainly white and mixed race minorities consider it their native language (this equals about 2.5% of the population). The rest of the population speak Shona and Ndebele, as well as other tribal languages. The Shona language is full of rich oral traditions. Many of these stories were collected in a novel, *Feso,* written by Solomon Mutswairo in the Shona language in 1956.

Since Zimbabwe sometimes experiences a shortage of food, the people are very grateful for what they have. They enjoy meat, particularly beef and chicken, as well as cornmeal which is used to prepare *sadza.* Sadza, or porridge, is made by mixing cornmeal and either water or milk together to make a thick paste. They usually eat sadza for lunch and dinner, along with meat and vegetables, such as spinach and beans.

For breakfast, the mother prepares a dish called *bota,* which is a thinner porridge than sadza and is flavored with peanut butter, butter, or jam. *Biltong* (beef jerky) and *boerewors* (beef sausage) are popular snacks. Since Zimbabwe is a former British colony, many people have adopted the British custom of having midday and afternoon tea.

In Your Classroom

Bring in beef jerky as a classroom snack.

Using cornmeal, jam and water or milk, make small servings of *bota* for your students.

Holidays & Festivals

Zimbabwe doesn't celebrate a great number of public holidays. Those that are recognized usually deal with the people and the history and culture of the country.

Independence Day
April 18
The first independence celebration was held at the Zimbabwe Grounds in 1980, and each year following celebrations are held in this stadium. Doves are released to symbolize peace, while fighter jets fly overhead. People sing the national anthem and the military and presidential family parade in the streets. The president lights a flame representing the nation's independence and gives a speech which is televised throughout the country.

Workers' Day
May 1
This day recognizes the contributions and impacts that working men and women of Zimbabwe have made.

Africa Day
May 25
This special celebration recognizes the 1963 founding of the Organization of African Unity, a charter between 30 African nations. Zimbabweans celebrate with the entire continent of Africa, remembering the unity of the land's people.

Heroes' Day
August
This day celebrates the many heroes of Zimbabwean history, known and unknown, big and small.

Armed Forces Day
August
Zimbabweans celebrate current and past members of their various armed forces, and recognize the sacrifices they have made throughout history.

Unity Day
December 22
This day celebrates the 1987 signing of the Unity Accord, which brought an end to a two decades-long conflict between two political parties.

Creative Arts

Art

Zimbabwe is made up of many ethnic groups, each with their own traditions and cultures. The largest of these ethnic groups is the Shona. They are known for using the best materials available, such as teak, to make intricate idols (carvings or sculptures of their gods.) They also use soapstone, serpentine, and a rare stone called verdite to make animal and human figurines. Many of their sculptors have become internationally known and have influenced many artists, particular African Americans.

Literature

Zimbabwe boasts a rich literary heritage. Chenjerai Hove, a Zimbabwean University graduate, is a famous essayist, poet, and novelist. Charles Mungoshi is famous for writing traditional stories and poems in both Shona and English. The novels *African Tears* and *Beyond Tears*, written by Catherine Buckle, have received international recognition. In these books, she talks about all she endured during President Mugabe's chaotic land redistribution. Ian Smith, the former Prime Minister of Rhodesia (before it became Zimbabwe) wrote two books, *The Great Betrayal* and *Bitter Harvest*. *The Grass is Singing*, the first novel written by Nobel Prize winner Doris Lessing, is set in Rhodesia.

Music

Zimbabwean music is a combination of folk and pop styles, borrowing from the old and the new to create a distinct national sound. The *mbira*, or thumb piano, is very important in Zimbabwean music. The most popular local music is called *sungura*. The genre caught on in a big way in the 1980s, and has grown and changed since. Some popular sungura artists past and present include The Khiama Boys, James Chimombe, and Leonard Zhakata.

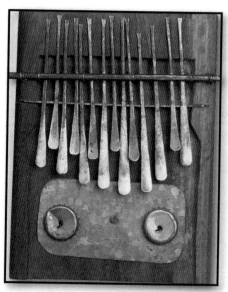

Mbira

In Your Classroom

Instead of carving soapstone, have the students carve soap! Ivory soap is the best type for carving. Give each student a bar and a sharp but safe object for carving, such as a toothpick, plastic knife or a rock. Encourage the students to carve birds, much like the one on the flag and those found at the Zimbabwe Ruins. To make it easier, show them how to first draw their design on their soap using a pen or pencil before carving into it. Put the finished bird carvings on display in your classroom.

Sports & Games

Football (soccer) is by far the most popular sport in Zimbabwe. Other sports, such as cricket and rugby, have a small following, and field hockey and swimming have become increasingly popular. The country won several medals in both field hockey and swimming in recent Olympic Games.

Kirsty Coventry, a Zimbabwean Olympic swimmer and world record holder, attended the University of Auburn in Alabama and swam competitively there. At the 2008 Beijing Olympics, Kirsty won one gold and three silver medals. In the Commonwealth Games and All-Africa Games she won a combination of 11 medals. The head of the Zimbabwean Olympic Committee called her, "our national treasure" and President Mugabe titled her "a golden girl."

Zimbabwe has also participated in Wimbledon and Davis Cup tennis competitions. The Black family—Wayne Black, Byron Black, and Cara Black—have been the most notable Zimbabwean competitors at those events.

Scouting is popular in Zimbabwe as well. This is an organization that teaches adolescent boys about woodcraft, exploration, tracking, fieldcraft, self-reliance and other survival skills. Thousands of Scouts learn these skills and put them into practice each year.

In Your Classroom

Teach the class basic survival skills, such as reading a compass or using the sun or stars to direct them. If any of the students are in the Boy Scouts, have them demonstrate or explain some of the skills they have learned.

Ask students to imagine they are planning a backpacking or camping trip. Have them write a list of all the things they will need to bring with them. Remind them to pack light. To make this more of a challenge, allow each student to bring only ten things to take along on the trip.

Answer Key

Egypt

Ancient Egyptian God and Goddesses (page 22)

1. Amun
2. Hathor
3. Nut
4. Geb
5. Shu
6. Osiris
7. Seth
8. Thoth
9. Horus
10. Isis
11. Anubis
12. Ra

Kenya

Speaking of Swahili... (page 43)

Conversations will vary, but here is a good example:

Character 1: Jambo.   (Hello.)
Character 2: Salama!   (Hello!)

1: Habari gani?   (How are you?)
2: Nzuri, asante.   (Fine, thank you.)

1: Jina lako nani?   (What is your name?)
2: Jina langu ni Abasi. Jina lako nani?   (My name is Abasi. What is your name?)
1: Dafina
2: Nafurahi kukuona, Dafina.   (Nice to meet you, Dafina.)
1: Asante.   (Thank you.)